TEACHING TECHNIQUES IN ENGLISH AS A SECOND LANGUAGE
Series Editors: Russell N. Campbell and William E. Rutherford

TECHNIQUES IN TEACHING VOCABULARY

Virginia French Allen

·OXFORD UNIVERSITY PRESS·

Oxford University Press

200 Madison Avenue
New York, N.Y. 10016 USA

Walton Street
Oxford OX2 6DP England

OXFORD is a trademark of Oxford University Press.

Library of Congress Cataloging in Publication Data
Allen, Virginia French.
Techniques in teaching vocabulary.
(Teaching techniques in English as a second
or foreign language) Includes index.
1. English language—Study and teaching—
Foreign students. 2. Vocabulary—Study and
teaching. I. Title. II. Series.
PE1128.A2A388   1982   428'.007'1   82-12519
ISBN 0-19-434130-5 (pbk.)

We would like to thank the following publishers for permission to reprint
material: the United States Information Agency; Oxford University Press,
Oxford; Longman Group Limited; Random House, Inc.; the Educational
Testing Service for sample questions from TOEFL.

Illustrations by Wendy Ann Fredericks and Steven Schindler.

Printed in Hong Kong

·EDITORS' PREFACE·

It has been apparent for some time that little attention has been given to the needs of practicing and student teachers of English as a Second Language.* Although numerous inservice and preservice teacher-training programs are offered throughout the world, these often suffer from lack of appropriate instructional materials. Seldom are books written that present practical information that relates directly to daily classroom instruction. What teachers want are useful ideas, suggestions, demonstrations, and examples of teaching techniques that have proven successful in the classroom—techniques that are consistent with established theoretical principles and that others in our profession have found to be expedient, practical, and relevant to real-life circumstances in which most teachers work.

It was in recognition of this need that we began our search for scholars in our field who had distinguished themselves in particular instructional aspects of second language teaching. We sought out those who had been especially successful in communicating to their colleagues the characteristics of language teaching and testing techniques that have been found to be appropriate for students from elementary school through college and adult education programs. We also sought in those same scholars evidence of

*In this volume, and in others in the series, we have chosen to use *English as a Second Language (ESL)* to refer to English teaching in the United States (as a second language) *as well as* English teaching in other countries (as a foreign language).

an awareness and understanding of current theories of language learning together with the ability to translate the essence of a theory into practical applications for the classroom.

Our search has been successful. For this volume, as well as for others in this series, we have chosen a colleague who is extraordinarily competent and exceedingly willing to share with practicing teachers the considerable knowledge that she has gained from many years of experience in many parts of the world.

Professor Allen's book is devoted entirely to the presentation and exemplification of practical techniques in the teaching of vocabulary. Each chapter of her book contains, in addition to detailed consideration of a wide variety of techniques, a number of activities that teachers can perform that tie the content of the book directly to the teachers' responsibilities in their classes. With this volume then, a critical need in the language teaching field has been met.

We are extremely pleased to join with the authors in this series and with Oxford University Press in making these books available to our fellow teachers. We are confident that the books will enable language teachers around the world to increase their effectiveness while at the same time making their task an easier and more enjoyable one.

Russell N. Campbell
William E. Rutherford

Editors' Note: Apologies are made for the generalized use of the masculine pronoun. It is meant to be used for simplicity's sake, rather than to indicate a philosophical viewpoint. We feel that the *s/he, her/him, his/her* forms, while they may be philosophically appealing, are confusing.

·CONTENTS ·

·CHAPTER ONE·
INTRODUCTION

Experienced teachers of English as a Second Language know very well how important vocabulary is. They know students must learn thousands of words that speakers and writers of English use. Fortunately, the need for vocabulary is one point on which teachers and students agree!

For many years, however, programs that prepared language teachers gave little attention to techniques for helping students learn vocabulary. Some books appeared to be telling teachers that students could learn all the words they needed without help. In fact, teachers were sometimes told that they ought *not* to teach many words before their students had mastered the grammar and the sound system of the language. In journal articles for teachers, vocabulary was seldom mentioned. Pronunciation and grammar were emphasized, but there was little or no emphasis on vocabulary. In short, vocabulary has been neglected in programs for teachers during much of the twentieth century. Perhaps we should try to understand why this is so.

REASONS FOR NEGLECTING VOCABULARY IN THE PAST

One reason why vocabulary was neglected in teacher-preparation programs during the period 1940–1970 was that it had been emphasized too much in language classrooms during the years before that time. Indeed, some people had believed it was the only key to

1

language learning. Learners often believed that all they needed was a large number of words. They thought they could master the language by learning a certain number of English words, along with the meanings of those words in their own language. Of course this belief was wrong. In addition to knowing English words and their meanings, one must know also how the words work together in English sentences. That is one reason for the emphasis upon grammar in teacher-preparation programs during the past few decades. During those years, teachers were told a great deal about new discoveries in English grammar. They heard much less about ways to help students learn words.

There is a <u>second</u> reason why so little was said in methodology courses about teaching words and their meanings. Some specialists in methodology seemed to believe that the meanings of words could not be adequately taught, so it was better not to try to teach them. In the 1950s, many people began to notice that vocabulary learning is not a simple matter. It is not simply a matter of learning that a certain word in one language means the same as a word in another language. Much more needs to be learned; and there were those who felt the complexities were too great to be dealt with in class.

According to an English/Spanish dictionary, for example, the words **garden** and **jardín** seem to have the same meaning. Each means a place where flowers are grown. But there are meanings of **garden** that do not correspond to the meanings of **jardín**. A garden is a place that may grow vegetables as well as flowers; whereas vegetables are grown in a **huerta** in Spanish, not in a **jardín**. This is just one of countless possible examples to show that vocabulary learning is not simply a matter of matching up words in the native language and the target language. Often those who prepared teachers gave the impression that vocabulary learning was so complex that one might better devote most of the class time to teaching the grammatical structures, with just a few vocabulary words, since students could not be given full and accurate understanding of word meanings in class. Indeed in some books and articles about language teaching, writers gave the impression that it was better not to teach vocabulary at all.

These, then, were some of the reasons for the general neglect of vocabulary in programs that prepared teachers—during a time when teachers were getting a good deal of help with other aspects of language instruction. We will summarize the reasons here:

1. Many who prepared teachers felt that grammar should be emphasized more than vocabulary, because vocabulary was already being given too much time in language classrooms.

2. Specialists in methodology feared students would make mistakes in sentence construction if too many words were learned before the basic grammar had been mastered. Consequently, teachers were led to believe it was best *not* to teach much vocabulary.

3. Some who gave advice to teachers seemed to be saying that word meanings can be learned *only* through experience, that they cannot be adequately taught in a classroom. As a result, little attention was directed to techniques for vocabulary teaching.

Each of those beliefs about vocabulary is true to a certain extent. It is true that too much time has been devoted to vocabulary in many classrooms. Often so much time goes into explaining the new words that there seems to be no time for anything else. That, of course, is unfortunate. Students who do not learn grammar along with vocabulary will not be able to use the language for communication. Even material in which all the words look familiar may be impossible to understand if the grammatical constructions have not been learned. The following paragraphs, for instance, contain very easy vocabulary; yet the meanings of the sentences cannot be grasped without a substantial knowledge of grammar:

> Things always know when a person isn't well. They know, but they just don't care. Many times, in little ways, things make life hard for people. They have special ways of doing this.
> When I'm not well, I can never find the things I need. The things I need have gone away from all the places where I look. That is one of the facts I have learned about people and things.

In classes where too little time is spent on grammar, students fail to learn how words are used in sentences; only the general *meaning* of a word is learned. Students learning the words **emphasize** and **emphasis**, for example, need more than an understanding of the area of meaning which those words represent. They should learn that **emphasis** is a noun, used like this, "We put **emphasis** on it." They should learn that **emphasize** is a verb, used like this, "We **emphasize** it." The noun use should be contrasted with the verb use, as follows:

There was not much **emphasis** on it. (Note the use of **on**.)
Few people **emphasized** it. (Note that **on** is not used.)

It is true, then, that students must learn grammar, which involves *uses* of words. It is never enough to learn only the words and their meanings. It is true that in some classrooms sentence construction has been given too little attention. It is also true that students will make mistakes if they learn the meanings of many words without learning how to put words together in sentences.

Furthermore, there is truth in the belief that experience is the best vocabulary teacher. Through experience with situations in which a language is used by speakers or writers, we learn that many of the meanings of a word do not correspond to the meanings of its so-called equivalent in another language. Since full understanding of a word often requires knowing how native speakers feel about what the word represents, some meanings cannot be found in a dictionary. It is necessary to know something about the customs and attitudes of native speakers if we are to know what words really mean to them.

Take the word **wall**, for instance. Every language has a word for the thing that English calls a wall. But how people feel about walls can be very different in different parts of the world, and those feelings are part of the meaning of the word. Suppose someone says, "Our new neighbors have built a wall around their property." In many countries, that statement would not surprise anyone. In those countries, it is customary to build a wall around one's property; most people do so. In most English-speaking communities, however, houses and gardens are usually visible from the street. To the native speaker of English, the building of the wall might suggest unfriendliness.

As we have seen, then, the learning of word meanings requires more than the use of a dictionary, and vocabulary acquisition is a complex process. Fortunately, however, teachers are being given more help with vocabulary teaching today.

REASONS FOR THE PRESENT EMPHASIS ON VOCABULARY

In teacher-preparation programs today, there is more attention to techniques for teaching vocabulary. One reason is this: In many ESL classes, even where teachers have devoted much time to vocabulary teaching, the results have been disappointing. Sometimes—after months or even years of English—many of the words most needed have never been learned. Especially in countries where English is not the main language of communication, many teachers want more help with vocabulary instruction than they used to receive.

Something else also accounts for today's concern with the learning of vocabulary. That is the fact that scholars are taking a new interest in the study of word meanings. A number of research studies have recently dealt with lexical problems (problems related to words). Through research the scholars are finding that lexical problems frequently interfere with communication; communication breaks down when people do not use the right words.

Such discoveries by scholars do not surprise classroom teachers. Teachers have never doubted the value of learning vocabulary. They know how communication stops when learners lack the necessary words. They do not believe that the teaching of vocabulary should be delayed until the grammar is mastered. In the best classes, neither grammar nor vocabulary is neglected. There is thus no conflict between developing a firm command of grammar and learning the most essential words.

Today, therefore, professional journals and teachers' meetings often reflect the current concern for more effective vocabulary teaching. When teachers come together for professional discussions, they raise such questions as these:

- Which English words do students need most to learn?
- How can we make those words seem important to students?
- How can so many needed words be taught during the short time our students have for English?
- What can we do when a few members of the class already know words that the others need to learn?
- Why are some words easier than others to learn?
- Which aids to vocabulary teaching are available?
- How can we encourage students to take more responsibility for their own vocabulary learning?
- What are some good ways to find out how much vocabulary the students have actually learned?

Answers to these and other questions will be found in the chapters that follow. The answers are based on the experience of teachers—teachers working in classrooms in many parts of the world.

If you and other teachers are using the book together, you will want to discuss the suggestions that the chapters offer. A major aim is to help experienced teachers recall successful techniques which they can share with colleagues newer to the field of ESL.

Whether or not you have had much teaching experience, you know a great deal about vocabulary learning. In your own study of other languages, you have discovered much about the learning of words. As you work through the activities proposed in each chapter, you will build on what you already know.

·CHAPTER TWO·

VOCABULARY LESSONS FOR THE FIRST STAGE

It has been said, "There is one English word that is known everywhere. The word is **cowboy**." This remark has a certain amount of truth. Such words as **rock star** and **cowboy** seem to be known by almost everyone (by almost every young person, at least). Indeed, such English words are usually learned without being taught, without being explained or drilled in class. All too often, however, a student who has easily acquired **cowboy** and **rock star** seems unable to master the words in the textbook, even after the teacher's explanations and drills. This is unfortunate, as experienced teachers know. Much of the vocabulary in English textbooks *must* be learned. Without it, no one can speak or understand the language. The question is what can teachers do while presenting the textbook words, so that students will learn them as well as **rock star** and **cowboy**.

In books that are intended for the first stage of English, the vocabulary lessons usually contain words for persons and things *in the classroom*, words like **boy**, **girl**, **book**, **pencil**, **window**, **door**. For teachers, and for authors of textbooks, it is easy to see why the beginning lessons should introduce such words. One reason is that the meanings can easily be made clear. Windows, walls, desks, and doors are things that the students can *see* while they are hearing the foreign names for them. Furthermore, things in the classroom can also be *touched*. This is important, because success in learning often depends on the number of senses which are used in the learning process. When students can touch something, in ad-

7

dition to hearing and seeing the word that names it, there is a stronger chance that the word will be learned. Even if there are practical reasons why each learner cannot touch the object, just seeing it while hearing its name is helpful. At least those two senses (sight and hearing) are working together to focus the learner's attention.

Teachers and textbook writers understand the value of lessons that introduce basic words, like the names of things found in classrooms and in the local community. They know that much of this vocabulary will be needed for defining more difficult words in later stages of the program. Moreover, much of the vocabulary found in lessons for beginners will be needed for writing and speaking English in future months and years. It is good to make an early start on such important words. Why, then, aren't they learned more easily?

WHY BASIC VOCABULARY MAY BE HARD TO LEARN

Why are students often slow to learn foreign words for familiar objects? To answer that question, we must look at vocabulary from the students' point of view. The students *already* have satisfactory words—in their own language—for everything in the classroom that they might want to name. They have been able to talk about such familiar objects for many years. Therefore, most members of the class feel no real need to learn other words for such things now. This is a problem that does not arise when words like **rock star** and **cowboy** are being acquired outside the classroom. (Those are words for new experiences that are not already named by words in the students' mother tongue.) But it is a problem to be solved when we teach the basic words that textbooks introduce. From the students' point of view, such words do not seem really necessary because words in the mother tongue serve all practical purposes.

There is something else to be noticed about vocabulary learning in and out of class. Let's imagine what happened years ago, when each of our students was learning words for familiar objects—words in the mother tongue. Quite probably, each word came to the child's attention as part of an experience that had special importance for him. Perhaps the words for **window** and **door** were learned when he heard an adult say (in the home language), "Grandma's gone, but we'll go to the **window** and wave goodbye," and "Daddy's here! Let's go to the **door** and let him in." Of course we don't know what really occurred on the day when the child learned those words in his own language, but one thing is sure. We do know that he was not told, for example, "Here are some words to learn. You will need them someday. The first word is **window. Window** means. . . ." Yet that is how vocabulary is often presented in the language class.

When we think about vocabulary lessons in this way, we become aware of five facts:

1. Foreign words for familiar objects and persons are important to teach, but we cannot expect most members of the class to learn them easily.

2. Teaching such words will require special skills because students often feel their native-language words for familiar objects and persons are all they *really need*.

3. Students are *very* likely to feel that foreign words for familiar objects are not really needed when the foreign language is not used for communication outside the language class.

4. When a student feels no real need to learn something, a feeling of need must be *created*—by the teacher.

5. To create in students' minds a sense of personal need for a foreign word, it is not enough to say, "Here is a word to learn." "Here is what the word means." "The word will be useful to you someday."

CREATING A SENSE OF NEED FOR A WORD

What is real need or personal need in relation to vocabulary learning? If a student feels he must learn certain words in order to please the teacher or to pass an examination, how real is that feeling of need? The need may indeed produce learning, especially among certain individuals and in certain cultures, but more often than not students who learn for such reasons—and for no other reasons—will gain little of permanent value. Among those who still cannot speak, write, or even read English after years of instruction, there are many with fine school records. They studied vocabulary in preparation for each examination during those years, and they answered the exam questions well; but their efforts did not produce the ability to communicate. There is more practical *command* of vocabulary among those who have needed English words for their own purposes (for communication in business or travel, or in friendships with speakers of English).

Of course it is usually not possible to create in a classroom the same conditions that produce successful vocabulary learning outside of school. It is especially impossible to create again the conditions that once helped our students learn fundamental vocabulary in their mother tongue. Nevertheless, it is useful to think about those conditions. When we have noticed certain facts about vocabulary learning outside of class, we can make some use of those facts while developing techniques for the classroom.

To see how this can be done, let's look at several words that are introduced in first-year textbooks, words representing nouns, verbs, and adjectives. Other kinds of words (such as prepositions, conjunctions, articles, and auxiliaries) are generally taught in the grammar lesson.

A LOOK AT A TEXTBOOK LESSON

Suppose we are about to teach from one of many textbooks where a vocabulary lesson looks more or less like this:

VOCABULARY

boy	door	girl	picture	wall
clock	floor	person	room	window

To the right of each listed word, we may find a corresponding word in the students' language. Somewhere on the page there may be a picture showing a boy and a girl in a room with a clock on one wall. With those aids to learning, the students will be expected to read (and perhaps to translate) the following sentences, which appear next in the textbook:

> This is a picture of a room. The room has a door
> and two windows. There is a clock on the wall. There
> are two persons in this room. The boy is sitting near the
> clock. The girl is sitting near the door.

That is how a page may look in a fairly typical textbook. As we consider techniques for teaching such a lesson—and as we compare it to vocabulary learning outside the school—we look first at the alphabetized list. What kind of help should we give students here? When words are learned *in the real world*, they are not met in alphabetical order. Early in the lesson, we must be prepared to take these words out of the list and to group together words that belong together in real life. This is not to say, of course, that alphabetical order can't serve other purposes. Without alphabetical order, for example, dictionaries and telephone directories would be useless. Even for a list of new words (as on our sample textbook page) alphabetizing may be appropriate in helping students to find a word during periods of study at home. At any rate, the alphabetized list is there, on the page. And if we consider it only one part of the lesson—if we are ready to move on quickly to other activities—the list does no harm. Let's consider techniques for dealing quickly with such a list.

WHAT TO DO ABOUT THE LIST
ON THE TEXTBOOK PAGE

Some teachers read aloud each word from the list while the students' books are closed. Other programs permit students to look at each word while the teacher is pronouncing it. Each procedure has advantages and disadvantages. Many times the sight of a word has a bad effect on students' pronunciation, as English spelling sometimes has little relation to the way the word sounds. Sometimes, however, pronunciation is considered less important than the rapid growth of vocabulary. At such times, students are encouraged to look at the word while hearing it pronounced, since learners tend to remember a word more easily if they see *and* hear it.

There is no harm in having students say each word after the teacher says it. Some students find it helpful; many enjoy saying the word as soon as they hear it. Hearing the word, seeing it, and saying it—all of these may be aids to learning. But they are only *part* of the learning process. More is needed, and the harm comes when there is no time for anything more. There are classes in which every student is asked to say every new word before anyone knows (or cares) how the word is used for communication. In such classes, too much time goes into this repeating of words *as words*.

When too much time is given to seeing and saying words (without relation to their normal use), too little time remains for more helpful activities. And as such, the alphabetized list of words at the top of our sample vocabulary page is not very conducive to that activity. Yet before leaving that list of words, let's think about ways of showing their meanings.

SHOWING THE MEANINGS OF WORDS

Everyone has seen English textbooks where meanings are shown in the students' mother tongue. In such books, the English word appears first, then the word in the students' language. In books without translations, the teacher is expected to provide a definition after reading aloud each English word. In classes where no one language is known by all the students, the teacher needs particular skill. The teacher must provide definitions in English, using words the class can understand. Vocabulary lessons for the first stage of English instruction (like the one we are describing now) use pictures for showing many meanings. In some classes for beginners, teachers use all three ways to show the meanings of vocabulary words:
1. pictures
2. explanations in the students' own language
3. definitions in simple English, using vocabulary that the students already know

In a later chapter we will consider other ways of showing meanings.

At this point it is worth noting something about these common kinds of vocabulary presentation. In all three cases teachers call attention to the meaning *after* calling attention to the English word. But let's think about that order of presentation. Is it really best to draw students' attention first to the new word and *then* to its meaning? It is interesting to compare this order with the order of events in the learning of vocabulary in one's mother tongue. During a child's early years, what happens first is this: the child has an *experience* with some object (perhaps a new toy truck). While his attention is on the truck, the child *then* hears the name of the object which has attracted his interest. (Perhaps some adult says, "What a nice **truck**!" or "Put away that **truck** and come to dinner.") First the child's attention is drawn to the truck; then the child gets the word that names it.

In second-language classes today, some teachers are trying to apply what has been discovered about the acquisition of first language vocabulary. Whenever possible, they offer their students some sort of experience with an object for which the English word will be taught. They try to draw students' attention to an object *before* spending much time on the English name for it.

Let's see how this might apply to our sample vocabulary lesson.

DRAWING ATTENTION TO MEANINGS BEFORE DRILLING WORDS

As we prepare to teach the textbook lesson, we look at the list of new words: **boy, clock, door, floor, girl, person, picture, room, wall, window.** We decide that there are at least two groups of related words here. One group contains words for people: **boy, girl, person.**

We think about ways of drawing students' attention to the *ideas* represented by those words (not to the words themselves). We consider a few possibilities and reject some. For instance, we *could* point to a boy and a girl in our class as a way of preparing

students to learn the words **boy** and **girl**. In some cultures, however, this procedure would produce discomfort, and a less personal way of demonstrating the meaning would be required.

   If the textbook has a picture that shows a boy and a girl, we
can direct attention to that picture. (Our sample textbook page has
such a picture.) To focus attention on the blackboard, however,
we may want to draw a set of illustrative stick figures there:

Notice that this is not a family group. These are persons, most of
them boys and girls. (We include pictures of men and women to
show that not all males are usually called boys, not all females are
called girls.)

If the English words **man/men**, **woman/women** have not already been taught, we do not need to introduce those words now. It is very possible, however, that the students will *request* the English words when they see the pictured men and women. When that happens, of course, we are delighted to supply those words; that is the perfect condition for learning vocabulary. It is also possible that some student in the class already knows the word **man** or **woman**. When that student offers the English word, many of his classmates will quickly learn it.

If we are totally unable (or unwilling) to draw, we can ask someone in the class to draw the set of stick figures on the blackboard before the lesson begins. (If the blackboard is small, and we need the space for other purposes, the pictures may be made on a very large sheet of paper. An advantage is that the paper can be saved for use again in a later lesson.)

At the beginning of the vocabulary lesson, we call students' attention to the set of stick figures. This can be done by pointing, or by covering one of the figures with a piece of paper, or by drawing a frame around the figures.

As soon as it appears that the students are paying attention, we give them the words that speakers of English use for such human beings. We point to one of the boys and say, "a boy" or "That is a boy." We point to another boy and again say, "a boy" or "That is a boy." In the same way, each of the girl figures is indicated and the word is given.

Below each of those figures we then write **a boy** or **a girl**. If we wish, we may also teach **a man** and **a woman** at this time. Certainly we will wish to do so if students express an interest in learning those words. Even if the English words for the pictured men and women are not taught now, however, the figures will serve a purpose: they will show that the words **girl** and **boy** do not usually represent adult persons.

Only a very short time (perhaps three minutes) should be given to this presentation of meanings and then of words. Now it will be important to give the students some experience with the *use of these words for communication*. It can be a very simple experience, but it must require the use of the word **girl**, **boy**, or **person** for giving and receiving information.

Communication Experience 1

The students are asked to take paper and pencil, and to see how many stick figures they can draw before the teacher says "Stop." (If the words **men** and **women** have not been taught, the students draw only boys and girls.) While the students are drawing, the teacher walks around the room and chooses a student who has made several particularly clear pictures. (We'll call him Mario.) The teacher asks him to come to the front of the room with his paper, which he does NOT show to any of his classmates.

> TEACHER: Mario has several persons in his picture. How many? How many boys are there? How many girls are there? Let's guess, *in English.*

As various students offer guesses (ten persons, four girls, three boys, five persons, six girls, etc.) Mario (and the teacher) look at his picture and accept the guess if it is correct. If the number is wrong, Mario corrects it. (For example: "No, *twelve* persons." "No, *six* girls." "No, *four* boys.") Finally, Mario shows his set of pictures to the class. If the figures are small and the class is large, he should copy the picture on the board while other students are telling the teacher about their own pictures. Before returning to his seat, Mario points to the figures he has drawn and—in English—says what they are.

Communication Experience 2

When there are both boys and girls in the classroom, the teacher writes the following dialog on the board, using names of girls in the class where blanks appear:

> THE FIRST SPEAKER: I'm thinking of a girl in this room. You have three guesses.
> THE SECOND SPEAKER: Are you thinking of____?
> THE THIRD SPEAKER: Are you thinking of____?
> THE FOURTH SPEAKER: Are you thinking of____?
> THE FIRST SPEAKER: I'm thinking of____.

The teacher shows how this dialog will be used for a game. First, the speakers are the teacher, who is thinking of some girl in the class, and three of the best students. After that, a *student* is the First Speaker, who thinks of a boy or a girl, and the dialog is used in a similar manner. If someone loses a guess by naming a *boy* when the players are trying to guess which *girl* is being thought of, the response to that guess will quickly teach both of these English words.

In classes where there are only boys, or only girls, it will still be possible to use this technique. The teacher introduces the dialog by indicating that the First Speaker is thinking of some person in *literature*—a boy or a girl in some story that everyone knows.

In this chapter we have noted the following points:

1. When we think about language learning in the classroom, it is useful to think also of ways in which people learn vocabulary *outside of school*. (Often such learning is very successful, for example, among persons who need a foreign language in business and among children learning their mother tongue.)

2. Vocabulary is best learned when someone feels that a certain word is *needed*.

3. Vocabulary for the first stage of ESL usually names certain things and persons in the classroom.

4. Although such vocabulary is essential, foreign words for familiar things may not *seem* really necessary to students, especially when English is not used outside their ESL class, because the words they already know in their mother tongue *satisfy any personal needs for communication*.

5. We can *make* the basic words in English necessary for communication. To do so, we engage students in activities that require those English words for the exchange of information or the expression of personal feelings.

6. The exchange of information by means of English words is possible even in classes for beginners.

✓ **7.** We can have simple communication experiences in the classroom if we make time for them.

✓ **8.** In some classes, the students spend a great deal of time saying English words without thinking (or caring) about the meanings. In such classes, time would be better spent on *meaningful use* of the words.

· ACTIVITIES ·

1. Observe a very young child who is just beginning to talk. How does the child learn words? Compare that process with procedures that are commonly used in language classrooms.

2. In many parts of the world, English words like **cowboy** and **rock star** are often learned without being taught. Find out (from some young students whom you know) what other words are learned without effort in your part of the world. How and why do you think they were learned?

3. A certain teacher sometimes complains, "Many of my students have not learned the English words **wall** and **window**, even though I always have students repeat each word after me several times." What might be the reason why the students have not learned those words?

4. Draw a set of stick figures that could be copied quickly on the blackboard to illustrate the meanings of **boy**, **girl**, **man**, **woman**, **house**, **tree**, **car**, **boat**, **box**, and **basket**.

5. When the textbook lesson begins with an alphabetical list, we need to take related words out of the list and prepare to teach those words in relation to each other. Here is an alphabetized list of words that might be found in a first-year lesson: **apple**, **ball**, **blue**, **chalk**, **curtain**, **page**, **round**, **sky**. Which of the words would you teach first, before the others in the list? Why?

6. Suppose you are ready to teach the words **circle**, **square**, and **triangle**. You want the students to think about the ideas which are represented by those words before you give them the English words for the ideas. Explain how you could do so.

7. Describe a simple classroom activity which would require the students to use the words **circle**, **square**, and **triangle** for the exchange of information.

·CHAPTER THREE·
MORE TECHNIQUES FOR BEGINNERS' CLASSES

We have seen (in Chapter 2) that understanding the meaning is only the first step in learning a word. It is a step that should take as little time as possible. Much more time should be given to other activities—activities which require students to *use* the new words for real communication.

Let's assume that we have shown our students the meanings of all the new words in our sample textbook lesson (**boy, girl, person, room, wall, floor, window, door, clock, picture**). Some meanings have been shown by pictures. For others (**wall, floor, window, door, clock**) we have pointed to something in our own classroom which is named by the English word. The students have heard and seen each of the words; they have copied the new vocabulary into their notebooks. In addition, they have used three of the new words (**boy, girl,** and **person**) in communication activities, as described in Chapter 2.

Now we are ready to engage the class in other experiences requiring the use of the new words. Here are a few of many possibilities:

1. The teacher introduces a very short dialog in which members of the class are identified according to their location (near the **door/window/clock**, etc.).

TEACHER: I'm thinking of a boy. He's near the **clock**.
A STUDENT: Are you thinking of____?

(After the dialog has been introduced by the teacher, it is used as follows: One student thinks of a classmate and mentions his or her location. The other students guess.)

2. The dialog is changed to include a review of colors and clothing (if words for these have been taught—and if the students are not wearing uniforms).

> TEACHER: I'm thinking of a girl in a **blue dress**.
> A STUDENT: Is she near the window?
> TEACHER: No. She's near the door.
> A STUDENT: Are you thinking of____?

3. Various students are asked to perform actions which demonstrate their understanding of the vocabulary—particularly **door**, **window**, **wall**, and **clock**. Members of the class (a few at a time) are asked to perform such actions as the following:

> Go to the **door**. Then go to a **window**.
> Touch the **wall** under the **clock**.
> Go back to your seats.

When the students have been at their seats for a long time and need a little physical activity, a good way to encourage learning of the new vocabulary words is to put them into simple commands. If the words **go**, **touch**, and **under** have not yet been taught, the meanings should be demonstrated by the teacher. Or the command which uses the unknown word may be spoken quietly—in the students' language—to two or three students who will perform the action first. Then the teacher repeats the command in English for the other students to hear and obey.

4. To put the word **floor** into a communication experience, there is a simple command that all members of the class can obey while sitting at their desks: "Touch the floor." This command can then be used for introducing additional words. One way of doing this is for the teacher to ask two or three students to occupy chairs at the front of the room, *with their backs to the rest of the class.* The teacher then asks them (first softly in their own language, then aloud in English) to demonstrate each of the following:

Touch the floor with one **hand**.
Touch the floor with **both** hands.
Touch the floor with your **right** hand.
Touch the floor **under your chair** with your right hand.

Notice that **left** is not introduced immediately after the word **right**. Even among adult native speakers of English, there are many who continue to confuse **right** with **left**. To reduce the chance of confusion it is usually wise to teach **right** thoroughly before introducing its opposite, **left**. (If—as often happens—the textbook presents both **right** and **left** in the same lesson, we can at least give more of the class time to the learning of **right**. Then, in a later lesson, we can come back to **left** for special practice.)

After several students have demonstrated comprehension of the new vocabulary by responding to the teacher's commands, individual members of the class take the role of the teacher. Each gives the same commands, which have been demonstrated, and classmates perform the actions. Besides offering practice in the use of the new vocabulary, the activity helps to keep students' minds alert.

WHY COMMANDS ARE USEFUL IN VOCABULARY CLASSES

When we ask students to respond physically to oral commands which use the new words, the activity is very much like what happens when one is learning one's mother tongue.

Each of us—while learning our own language—heard commands and obeyed them for many months before we spoke a single word. Even after we started to talk, it was a long time before we mastered the words and constructions that we heard from adults. Nevertheless, we could *understand* the adults' commands; we could and did respond to commands like "Go to your toy box and get your new fire engine—the one with the wheel that you broke yesterday—and take it to Grandpa."

Children have frequent experiences in obeying commands during the early years of learning the mother tongue. Those experiences appear to play an important part in the learning of vocabulary. Comparable experiences should be provided in the second-language classroom for students of all ages.

We have been considering words for things and persons in the classroom—the kinds of words generally found in textbooks for beginners in English. We have suggested ways of making such words appear necessary and important. We have mentioned the value of giving students the English word *after* they have begun to think about the object or action or situation which the word represents.

When students have observed an action—touching, for example—and have wondered what the action is called in English, it is not difficult to teach them the word **touch**. For mastery of the word, we can then ask the class to obey simple commands that contain **touch**; the commands are given first by the teacher, then by selected students.

USING REAL OBJECTS FOR VOCABULARY TEACHING

For helping students understand the meaning of a word, we often find that a picture is useful, if it is big enough to be seen by all members of the class. But *real objects* are better than pictures whenever we have them in the classroom. When there are real windows, doors, walls, floors, desks, and clocks in the classroom, it is foolish not to use them in our teaching. But in some classes, unfortunately, the students seem never to be asked to look at them, point to them, walk to them, touch them. Only the textbook pictures are used. This is a waste of excellent opportunities. In most cases, a picture of something is less helpful than the thing itself.

There are a *few* exceptions, however. The exceptions include articles of clothing. Shoes, shirts, skirts, dresses, etc., are usually present in the classroom; but when we show meanings of such words we should be careful about calling attention to clothing which is worn by members of the class. Such attention may make the wearer feel uncomfortable.

   This problem does not usually arise with less personal kinds
of objects: eyeglasses, sunglasses, wallets (or billfolds), handbags,
umbrellas. Several of these can often be found in the classroom;
other objects can be brought to class easily enough: a can opener, a
pair of scissors, a box of paper clips, a toothbrush, a bar of soap,
buttons of many colors and sizes and of various materials. The
general recommendation is this: For showing the meaning of an
English noun, use the real object whenever possible.

   There are exceptions to the recommendation for real objects,
however. These exceptions include (1) clothing that members of
the class are wearing, and (2) words like **man, woman, boy,** and
girl. In many situations, it seems awkward to point to individual
members of the class while saying, "He's a boy; she's a girl."
Pictures of persons, or stick figures (drawn by the teacher or a
student) are more suitable.

   For similar reasons, teachers often prefer to use pictures for
introducing words that name *parts of the body*. The best sort of
picture for this purpose is a simple, impersonal line drawing:

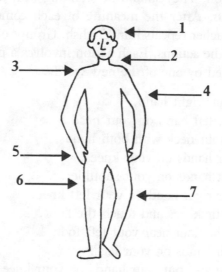

Notice that an arrow has been drawn to each part which is to be
named, and each arrow is numbered. Notice also that the English
names for the parts do not appear on the drawing yet.

On the day when such words are to be learned, the teacher
(or a member of the class) makes a large copy of the drawing on
the blackboard. The students are given a minute to look at the
drawing, and to copy it—and also to wonder what the English
words for the parts of the body are.

Now they are ready to learn that arrow 1 points to the *head*.
The teacher says the word and writes it above the arrow beside 1.
As each part is named, the student writes the English word on the
numbered arrow on his copy of the drawing.

This is the first step toward learning English names for the
parts of the body. But it is only the first step. We have not yet
created in the student's mind a feeling of *need* for each of those
English words. We have not convinced him that it is important to
learn a new word for something he can already name in his mother
tongue. For that purpose, we may again use a series of commands.
(Each should begin with **please** if we wish to demonstrate cour-
tesy while teaching vocabulary.) Commands are given—perhaps
first in the students' language, quietly, to one or two who demonstrate the action. They should be standing with their *backs to the
rest of the class*. After the meaning of each command has been
shown, the teacher repeats it in English. Groups of students stand
and perform the actions. Each action involves a part of the body
which is named by one of the new words:

> Raise your right hand.
> Put your left hand on your head.
> Touch your neck with both hands.
> Put your hands on your knees.
> Put both hands on your shoulder.
> Put your right hand on your left knee.
> Bend your knees and touch the floor.
> Touch the floor near your left foot.
> Put both hands on your legs.
> Sit down and put your hands on your knees.

For practice in *saying* the new words, a number of students
may be asked to play the teacher's role, giving the commands.
Even those who do not actually say the words, however, benefit

from this kind of experience. They have many opportunities to associate familiar actions with the English words that name them. Furthermore, it becomes *important* to the student to notice whether he hears **neck** or **knee**, for example, when a command is given.

OTHER COMMUNICATION EXPERIENCES FOR THE CLASSROOM

There are many other ways to create a communication situation in the classroom, of course. Suppose we have used a picture that shows a head with its various parts: hair, eyes, ears, nose, mouth. Those parts have been named in English; the students have printed the names in their notebooks with their copies of the picture. Now the stage is set for an experience in which students use those English words to *communicate*. The activity may go like this:

First the teacher introduces the topic of life on other planets, using a few pictures and (if necessary) a few sentences in the students' language. The students are then told that they are going to read about a visitor from another planet. Their job is to draw a picture of the visitor, *according to the sentences which they are going to read*. For example, if they read that the imaginary visitor has two heads, they must draw two heads. No one should look at a classmate's drawing. They will have five minutes for reading the description and drawing the picture. (If students cannot read English, the description should be read for them by the teacher.)

Each student takes a pencil and a blank sheet of paper on which to make his drawing. The description of the visitor (which the teacher had previously printed on a large sheet) is taped to the wall, and the students begin the task.

The sentences that describe the visitor may be these:

I have a friend from Mars. My friend has a big head. He has three eyes. He does not have hair. In place of hair, he has five ears. His five ears are on top of his head. His neck is very long. His mouth and his two noses are in his long neck. Please draw a picture of this visitor from Mars.

During the time allowed for this activity, the teacher walks around the room, observing the work of the students. One student is asked to copy his drawing on the blackboard, while the teacher reads the description aloud. The drawing is discussed. Does it fit the description? The teacher's own drawing (made before class, on a large sheet) is displayed. There is a discussion (in English) of differences between the students' drawings and the teacher's model.

For homework, each student may make a *different* drawing which represents an imagined visitor from another planet—his own idea of such a visitor. He is then to write a description of his visitor (in English) and bring it to class with his drawing. After the descriptions have been corrected by the teacher, each student tries to make a drawing which fits a classmate's description. His classmate judges the accuracy of the drawing compared with the sentences which describe the visitor.

THE VALUE OF PICTURES THAT STUDENTS DRAW

In several of the techniques which have been mentioned, pictures are made by students. Many teachers like to use pictures the students themselves have made. Such pictures have certain advantages.

1. They cost little or nothing.
2. They are available even in places where no other pictures can be found.
3. They do not require space for storing and filing as pictures from other sources do.
4. Sometimes students who are poor language-learners can draw well. Exercises which require drawing will give such students a chance to win praise, and the praise may help those students learn.
5. When someone has drawn a picture of a scene, he knows the *meanings* of the English words that the teacher will use while talking about parts of his scene. The meanings are in his mind before he is given the English word. (As we have noted, meanings often come before words in successful learning of vocabulary.)

Fortunately much of the basic vocabulary represents things which are easy to draw—even when the student (or teacher) is not an artist. Most people can draw well enough to show meanings of **house**, **church**, **tree**, **flower**, **cloud**, **moon**, **mountain**, and **star**. Even the least artistic teacher can draw pictures to represent the words **flag**, **dish**, **cup**, **glass**, **ladder**, and **key**. If the teacher prefers not to make pictures, there is almost always some member of the class who will enjoy doing so. Young students are especially fond of drawing—particularly when they are permitted to draw on the blackboard.

Here is a way to use students' artistic talents for the introduction of new vocabulary. Two students who like to draw are asked to go to the blackboard. The teacher explains that these two helpers will draw some pictures for the class, and that the teacher will give the English word for each picture after it has been drawn. Each of the two helpers—working side-by-side—draws a series of pictures, as instructed by the teacher, who whispers directions (in the students' language if necessary). For example, the teacher's whispered instructions may be as follows, "two or three trees, a few clouds, the sun, a few birds, a mountain, a house, a ladder against a wall of the house, a tent, a flag on the tent."

After each of these has been drawn by both helpers, the teacher gives the English word for what was pictured, and it is copied into notebooks by members of the class. When the scene is completed, the helpers, whom we'll call Paul and Henri, take their seats. Another student is asked to come to the blackboard. His job is to point to any part of either picture which is mentioned during the following conversation:

TEACHER: I see three **clouds** in Paul's picture. (*The student at the board points to them*.) What do *you* see?
A MEMBER OF THE CLASS: I see four **birds** in Henri's picture. (*The student at the board points*.)

The conversation is continued, by various students, until all parts of both pictures have been mentioned and pointed to.

The techniques described in this chapter encourage students to use new vocabulary through such activities as the following:

- guessing games in which members of the class are identified by location and by clothing
- actions that are performed in response to commands
- drawing of pictures by students to match English descriptions
- discussions of pictures drawn by members of the class

Such techniques require no special equipment or material, and they give students personal reasons for feeling that English words for familiar objects are good to know.

·ACTIVITIES·

1. Write a dialog that could introduce a guessing game (similar to 2 on page 22) in which the players use English words for colors, clothing, and parts of the classroom (**wall**, **window**, **clock**, etc.).

2. Write a series of commands (similar to 3 on page 22) that would require students to understand the following words: **hand**, **head**, **face**, **ear**, **neck**, **back**, **foot** (**feet**).

3. Write a series of commands which all members of a class could obey without leaving their seats. The commands should contain basic vocabulary and require *physical* actions.

4. It is better to point to the real desks and windows in the classroom than to use a picture of desks and windows for showing meanings of English words. However, *some* meanings should probably be shown through pictures. In which of the following might it be better to use pictures instead of touching or pointing to examples in the class? Under what circumstances would pictures be preferable: **nose**, **dress**, **shoes**, **blackboard**, **map**, **clock**, **watch**, **leg**, **wall**?

5. Page 25 lists many objects (scissors, buttons, etc.) that can easily be brought to the classroom to show meanings of vocabulary. Add five more readily available objects to that list.

6. Write a very simple description of an imaginary visitor from another planet. Then write instructions to tell students how to use

31

the description for the picture-drawing activity on page 27.

7. Draw simple pictures to illustrate meanings of five of the following words: **house, tree, flower, sun, moon, star, flag, cat, cup, ladder, wheel, snake, fish.**

8. Suppose you have students in your vocabulary class who like to draw pictures. Make a list of ten things you could ask them to draw on the blackboard for a review of English vocabulary. (Include some phrases, like **a few clouds above a mountain, a flag on a pole beside a house.**)

·CHAPTER FOUR·
SPECIAL USES OF VISUAL AIDS

Chapters 2 and 3 have emphasized the value of visual aids in teaching vocabulary (especially in beginners' classes). Successful language learning outside the school is generally in a situation where the learner can *see* what is named by the word to be learned. Whenever possible, that condition of successful vocabulary learning should be provided in second-language classrooms.

We have noted that visual aids are available in many forms. We have considered several that require little or no time or expense to prepare. When students see actions performed by a classmate or two in response to the teacher's instructions, that is a kind of visual aid. When we point to parts of the classroom, or bring into the classroom readily accessible objects—boxes, bottles, can openers, scissors, light bulbs, candles, tools, or small toys—we are using visual aids. (The sense of touch can be added to the sense of sight, in order to strengthen the association between the object and the English word, when various students touch and hold the objects being named.) This chapter will suggest additional ways to prepare and use various kinds of aids to encourage vocabulary learning.

PREPARING AND USING PICTURES

Pictures for vocabulary teaching come from many sources. In addition to those drawn by the students (or by the teacher) there are attractive sets which are intended for schools. Pictures which have

been cut out of magazines and newspapers are also useful; many
inexpensive books for children have attractive pictures which
show meanings of basic words.

Often a picture will show a situation or a scene in which there
are several different things and persons. It is good for students to
see the total scene or picture—to see how its parts are related to
the whole. It is also helpful (especially for beginners in English) to
see a picture of a single object or person as the only focus of attention.

Suppose, for example, we have a picture of each of the following: a church, a taxi, a bus, a traffic light, a policeman, a mailbox. Suppose each of the pictures is large enough to be seen by all
in the class. The students have seen and heard the English word
for each one, and have copied the word into their notebooks. Our
aim now is to help the students master the vocabulary, so we want
to encourage the use of each word for communication. We consider possible techniques for making students feel it is important
to know the English word. Here is one way:

1. The teacher arranges the pictures along the ledge of the blackboard, saying something like this: "We'll put the taxi here. That's
the first picture. Then the bus . . . then the traffic light . . . then
the church . . . then the policeman . . . then the mailbox."

2. The teacher asks a member of the class (We'll call him Lee) to
come to the blackboard.

> TEACHER: Lee is going to move one of the pictures for
>   us. We're going to tell him which picture to
>   move. Lee, please move the policeman. Put
>   the policeman first. (*Lee moves the picture of
>   the policeman, placing it first in the row on the
>   ledge of the blackboard.*)
> TEACHER: Put the taxi first. (*Lee does so.*)

3. The teacher indicates that various members of the class should
request Lee to make other changes in the order of the pictures—
using English, of course. For example:

A STUDENT: Move the church. Put the church first.
> (*Lee does so.*)

A STUDENT: Move the mailbox, *etc.*

If the class has begun to learn the ordinal numerals (**first, second, third,** etc.) these may be reviewed in connection with this activity. After each rearrangement of the pictures, the teacher (and then various students) say: "Now the ____ is first; the ____ is second; the ____ is third."

In the activity which has just been described, students use English words while talking about changes in location of pictures and changes in relationships. To make such changes quickly and easily, we need pictures that can be moved and rearranged without taking time to pin them or tape them to the wall. The pictures can be arranged on the ledge of the blackboard, as suggested; but there is another very easy way of arranging them for temporary display. It requires only the following:

• about three yards of cotton flannel (also called outing flannel)—cloth with a matted, fluffed surface. (Flannel is used for infant care, so it is found wherever cloth is sold.)
• scissors and paste or glue

DIRECTIONS

Cut this large piece of flannel into two equal parts. One half will be used as background against which pictures will be displayed. Tape that half to the wall near the blackboard, where it can remain permanently and be seen by all members of the class. (If you wish, the edges of the cloth may be hemmed to make a neater appearance. Tan or gray flannel has the advantage of looking clean longer, but ordinary white outing flannel serves just as well. The important requirement is the matted, fluffed surface, which all cotton flannel has.)

Using the other half of the cloth, cut out small pieces of it and glue or paste them to the backs of pictures. Use only a *little* glue or paste, and *small* pieces of cloth. A scrap of flannel that is about one-fourth as large as the picture should be enough.

When a small scrap of flannel has been attached to the back of a picture, it will hold the picture against the flannel background. You will not need tape, tacks, or pins. Flannel sticks to flannel, so the pictures will not fall off the flannel background. They will remain in place for several minutes.

The flannelgraph (as this simple device is sometimes called) provides a convenient means of encouraging students to use new vocabulary, while also reviewing grammar. Prepositions like **near**, **beside**, and **between** are easily reviewed when we arrange and rearrange pictures with the flannelgraph, as are verb changes like **is/was** and **are/were**. For instance, the students can be led to talk about the pictures in this way:

• There **are** three things **between** the mailbox and the traffic light now.
• There **was** a bus **near** the church, but there **is** a taxi **near** the church now.

It takes very little time (or money) to produce a flannelgraph. Often students enjoy helping with the cutting and pasting of the flannel pieces; and that experience itself can result in language learning when the teacher talks to the helpers in English about what is happening. ("That piece of flannel is big enough." "Don't use too much glue." "Now let's cut some pieces of flannel to put behind this picture.") Such an experience does much to teach vocabulary.

Long-term Displays of Pictures

Flannelgraphs are extremely useful for *temporary* arrangements of pictures, but something else is needed for permanent or long-term displays. When the class meets regularly in the same room, much of the wall space ought to be used for pictures that show meanings of important words. There should be a set of pictures illustrating family groups, another set showing animals, others showing buildings of various kinds. In other displays there should be pictures of furniture, means of transportation, workers in various occupations, shapes (triangles, rectangles, circles, squares).

Not all of these can or should be shown at the same time. Each should remain on the walls long enough to be noticed and to become familiar to members of the class.

There are several ways to encourage students to notice the wall displays:

1. Certain students can be asked to help in preparing the display, deciding which words should be printed below the pictures, and then printing the captions.

2. Frequently the class can be given such assignments as the following:

• Look at the pictures on the back wall and find five red things in those pictures. Write the English names for those five red things.
• In the pictures on the walls, find five things with wheels. Write the English names for those five things.
• In the pictures on the walls, find ten things that belong to a house. Write their English names.
• Look at the picture that is near the back window. There are many people in the picture. Which of the following would be the best title for the picture? (Explain why.)

> Visiting the Zoo
> Learning to Ride a Bicycle
> Waiting for a Bus

VISUAL AIDS FOR TEACHING VERBS

Demonstrating an action is the best way of teaching meanings of many verbs. To teach the word **walk**, for instance, we start walking toward another part of the classroom. When it appears that the students are paying attention (and wondering about the purpose of our action), we say, while continuing to walk, "I'm walking . . . walking. What am I doing, class? Say, 'You're walking.' "

Notice what the teacher does NOT say while in the process of walking. The teacher does *not* say, "I walk." At this stage in their learning, the students should not associate the one-word present tense form (**walk**) with an action that is occurring at the moment of speaking. When we draw their attention to an action that is happening while we are speaking, it is more helpful to use the *progressive* verb form (with **-ing** after **am, is,** or **are**).

Actions like walking, standing, pointing, and touching are easy to demonstrate in class. The meanings of other verbs can be shown through simple dramatic presentations. Even teachers with no dramatic ability can mime certain actions well enough to show the meanings of verbs like **eat, drink, laugh,** and **smile.**

Pictures are very useful for showing the meanings of verb *phrases* (**is running, is jumping, are playing football, are walking in the park**). Pictures do not offer the best way of introducing the single-word verb forms like **jump, play,** or **walk.** When native speakers describe what they see in a picture, they are more likely to say "The boy is walking" than "The boy walks."

To introduce the meaning of a verb, it is easy and helpful to use commands. Meanings of more than 100 essential verbs can be introduced through commands. Students can learn several of them when the entire class responds to the following series:

> Stand (up).
> Raise your hands.
> Touch your shoulders.
> Clap your hands.
> Stop.

The teacher gives each command to one or two leaders—speaking quietly and using their language if necessary. The command is then spoken more loudly by the teacher, in English, and the students perform the action. After two or three repetitions of the series, there is usually at least one member of the class who is ready to give the same commands—in English—to his classmates.

A VISUAL AID FOR TEACHING ADVERBS

Many adverbs are best taught in the *grammar* lesson, not the vocabulary lesson. Words like **now, then,** and **already** are usually taught while students are learning distinctions between present tense and past tense, or between past and present perfect. Words like **always, never, often,** and **seldom** are other adverbs that are generally taught in relation to grammar, as they show the frequency with which an action occurs.

There are, however, many adverbs that can easily be taught in the vocabulary class when we use a visual aid: a demonstration of an action.

Suppose, for instance, that the students have learned to respond to a command like "Walk to the door." We now add an **-ly** adverb: "Walk to the door **slowly**." A little later, **quickly** can be introduced. (To avoid confusion, it is wise *not* to teach words with opposite meanings, like **slowly** and **quickly**, at the same time.) There is a special advantage to be gained by delaying the introduction of **quickly** until the students have mastered **slowly**. The advantage is that the students then feel a real need to learn the word **quickly**. They have wanted such a word, and now the word is provided. This is the ideal condition for vocabulary learning.

Using Student Helpers

In situations where mimed actions by teachers are not considered proper, a student may be selected to serve as helper. In most classes there are students who are natural actors. They enjoy performing certain imaginary actions for classmates. The teacher asks one such student (first in his own language, if necessary, then immediately in English) to pretend to eat, drink, smile, laugh, wave, swim, sleep, brush your teeth, comb your hair, wash your face, fly like a bird, drive a car. (These are just a few possibilities for miming actions to show meanings.)

When a student is asked to mime three or four such actions during a lesson, his classmates may soon wish to join in the actions. (English words for the actions should always be used in the commands.)

Later, when the students have learned to use the progressive verb forms (with **-ing** and **am, is,** or **are**) the class will be ready for the following experience in communication:

Selected students come to the front of the classroom. Each draws a slip of paper. On each slip there is a command which requires miming an action (a command which the class has heard and responded to before). The commands may include "Climb a ladder," "Comb your hair," "Telephone someone," etc.

Each student looks at the slip which he has received, then performs the requested action. While he is miming the action, his classmates try to guess what he is pretending to do. ("Are you dancing?" "Are you opening a door?" "Are you climbing a ladder?") The guesses, of course, must be expressed in English.

Many teachers have used this technique successfully. (That is equally true of the other techniques that are described in this book.) As we all know, however, different situations have different requirements. Learners are not the same everywhere; neither are teachers. Some teachers feel uncomfortable about using certain techniques that other teachers find easy and helpful.

If a reader thinks, "I could never do *that* in *my* class," there may indeed be reasons why the suggested activity would not be suitable. In that case, it will be important to understand the *purpose* of the activity, and then to think, "What *could* be done to reach that goal?"

Suppose, for example, English is being taught where neither the teacher nor any student is able or willing to mime actions like swimming, flying, or driving a car. It is still possible to have certain students perform actions like the following, for demonstrations of verb meanings:

> Walk to the blackboard.
> Take a piece of chalk.
> Draw a large circle.
> Divide it into two parts.
> Write the first letter of the alphabet below the circle.
> Return to your seat.

Many of these commands are not very different from the directions which language teachers regularly give their students during class periods. Students frequently receive and obey the following requests, among others:

> Please sit down.   Write your name.
> Open your books.   Listen.

Turn to page ＿＿.	Answer.
Copy these words.	Repeat.
Read aloud.	Try again.
Begin.	Share your book with ＿＿.
Stop.	Pass your papers to the
Wait.	front of the room.

Even in beginners' classes, such everyday routine commands should always be given in English after the first few days. There is no good reason for giving routine commands in the students' language after the meanings have been made clear. To do so is to waste valuable chances for helping students learn.

In Chapters 2, 3, and 4 we have considered ways of teaching the kinds of vocabulary that should be learned during the first stage of English instruction. Various techniques have been described in relation to these points:

1. People are best able to learn a word when they feel a personal *need* for that word.

2. Teachers can *create* in students' minds the feeling that certain English words are needed.

3. To produce that sense of need, it is *not* enough just to mention an English word and give students its meaning.

4. Understanding, hearing, and seeing a word are only first steps toward knowing it.

5. Those first steps should be followed by activities that require students to *use* the new words for communication.

We have mentioned several ways to show the meaning of an English word, through such aids as the following:

1. objects already in the classroom

2. objects that can easily be brought to class (umbrellas, scissors, tools, buttons of many colors and sizes, etc.)

3. drawings by the teacher and drawings by students

4. pictures from magazines and newspapers (as well as from commercial sources)

5. demonstrations to show actions

In connection with various techniques and materials, we have noted the value of using students as helpers—to draw pictures, to prepare displays for the classroom walls, to mime actions (performing imagined acts like telephoning, brushing teeth, driving a car).

In these chapters, the emphasis has been on experiences which require students to use English words for communication. In some of the suggested activities, the new words are used for *making something happen*. (An action is performed, or a picture is drawn, according to directions that are given in English.) In other activities, English is used for *giving and receiving information*. For instance, students find out, by using English, what a classmate is doing or they guess which pictures a classmate has drawn.

The instructional value of such activities is this: when someone has to accomplish something which can be done only by using certain words, those words will be learned.

The next chapter will consider techniques for teaching students at the Intermediate level of English. At that level, students continue to need some of the same kinds of experiences which are needed by beginners. However, there are some new needs, too. Furthermore, techniques for Intermediate classes can make use of the vocabulary which has already been taught in the lessons of Stage I.

·ACTIVITIES·

1. From a magazine or an inexpensive book for children, obtain five pictures that show meanings of words which first-year students of English should learn (words like **house**, **car**, **tree** . . .). Each picture should be large enough to be seen by all members of your class. Attach each picture to a piece of cardboard or stiff paper. Describe an exercise (similar to the one on page 34) in which the five pictures are arranged and rearranged on the ledge of the blackboard (or taped to the board).

2. Make a flannelgraph, following the directions on page 35. Prepare five pictures for use with the flannelgraph. (Each picture should show just one object or person.) Explain how you could use the pictures and the flannelgraph for teaching certain nouns, adjectives, and prepositions.

3. Collect several pictures that could be displayed on your classroom walls, and group them to show kinds of animals, kinds of vehicles, furniture, buildings, and workers in various occupations. Put each group into a separate folder or large envelope.

4. Write three assignments (similar to those described on page 37) which would encourage students to look carefully at certain pictures which you collected for Activity 3 (above).

5. Write a description of a lesson in which meanings of the following are taught:
• Write your name.

• Walk slowly to the back of the room.
• Telephone a friend.

6. Suggest three ways in which students can serve as helpers in the classroom, and explain how the helpers could learn vocabulary from those experiences.

7. List ten directions or instructions (such as "Open your books") which students in your class should hear—in English—during every lesson.

·CHAPTER FIVE·
TEACHING VOCABULARY IN INTERMEDIATE CLASSES

What is an *Intermediate* class? In English as a Second Language, the terms *Advanced* and *Elementary* are easier to define. Advanced students are those who understand most of what they hear and read in the language class, although they still need help with material intended for native speakers of English. The term *Elementary* applies to beginners—at any age.

Advanced and *Elementary* are as different as black and white (as anyone who has taught on both those levels could say). But *Intermediate* has much in common with each—just as there are elements of both black and white in the color gray. Consequently, there is no clear line between Elementary and Intermediate vocabulary.

At the Intermediate level, we teach many of the same kinds of words that Elementary students need. Like lessons for beginners, the Intermediate vocabulary lessons include many words for things and persons in the learners' daily lives. There is much that the two levels have in common.

Compared with beginners, however, Intermediate students have one great advantage. They have learned a large number of English words which can now be used by the teacher for defining new vocabulary. Defining English words by means of other English words requires real skill. It is a skill that is particularly needed by teachers of Intermediate classes, for two reasons. One reason is this: As a general rule, Intermediate students should hear *only* English from their teacher. Even in programs where the learners' native language is sometimes used in teaching beginners, the classes for Intermediate students should be conducted entirely in English. And they can be, if the teacher has learned to make explanations that use vocabulary already known to the class.

There is another reason why teachers of Intermediate classes need skill in composing simple English explanations. Unlike most of the basic vocabulary that is taught in Elementary lessons, much of the Intermediate vocabulary cannot be demonstrated through actions or shown through pictures. However, we can usually show the meanings of Intermediate-level words by putting them into English explanations where the *other* words in the sentences are already known.

USING SIMPLE ENGLISH TO SHOW MEANINGS OF WORDS

Let's take the word **parent**, for example. The meaning of **parent** can be made clear to students who already know the words **person, mother**, and **father**. We can put **parent** into a defining sentence like this, "A parent is a person's mother or father." Notice that it is the teacher—not the student—who provides the defining sentence. Defining words by means of other words is a technique needed by teachers. It is a skill that is also acquired by some students; but the ability to give a definition—or a synonym—is less important than the ability to use the word for communication. Many native speakers with a full command of English vocabulary have little skill in *defining* the words that they use.

Defining English words by means of *simpler* English words is not easy. Skill in the use of the technique generally requires considerable experience in teaching English to speakers of other languages. Through repeated contacts with learners at various levels, one discovers which words an Intermediate student may be expected to know.

Fortunately, there is an excellent source of help: a book which is known as a learner's dictionary. Two learner's dictionaries are well known: the *Oxford Student's Dictionary of American English* and the *Longman Dictionary of Contemporary English*. To appreciate the helpfulness of a learner's dictionary, compare these two definitions of an English verb which is often taught at the Intermediate level—the verb **drown**:

1. From a learner's dictionary—**to drown**: to die by being under water for a long time.
2. From a standard dictionary intended for English-speaking people—**to drown**: to be suffocated by immersion in water or other liquid; to sink and perish in water.

For Intermediate students of English, several of the words used in definition (2) are at least as difficult as the word which is being defined. Therefore a definition like (2) cannot be helpful. In (1), the words of the definition are quite sure to be known by students in an Intermediate class.

It is true that a definition like (1) is less exact, less complete, than definitions which are prepared for native speakers. However, such a definition is enough to *introduce* the meaning. (At first introduction, one cannot know everything about a new friend. One learns more from every experience with the new human acquaintance—or the new word.)

More will be said in Chapters 8 and 9 about the students' use of dictionaries. For our present purposes, the point is this: an English dictionary which has been specially prepared for learners of ESL is an essential tool for *teachers*, especially those teaching Intermediate and Advanced vocabulary.

THE VALUE OF SEEING A NEW WORD IN A SENTENCE

At the Intermediate level, a learner's dictionary can show teachers how to explain "new" words by means of the English words the students are most likely to know. Furthermore, such dictionaries usually give helpful example sentences in addition to definitions. An example sentence for **drown** might be, "The dead boy's mother was very sad after her son **drowned** in the river." Often an example sentence can help the student more than a definition. No definition is needed for the verb **contain** (which is generally taught at the Intermediate level) when the students are given example sentences like the following:

> These boxes **contain** chalk.
> That bottle **contains** water.
> Handbags often **contain** money and many other things.

Although no definition or synonym for **contain** has been given here, the meaning of the word should be clear to students who have already learned the other words in the example sentences.

Such sentences are helpful to all students. They have a special usefulness when we are teaching students whose home language is related to English. For those students, an example sentence can say, in effect, "The word which is introduced in this example is very much like a word in your language; and their meanings are very similar." On the other hand, where the meanings of similar-appearing words are different, the example sentence can call attention to the difference.

In Spanish, French, Dutch, and German, for instance, there are many words that look very much like English words and that have the same origin. Such words are called *cognates*. Yet the usual meaning of the English word may be quite different from the meaning of the cognate in another language. A series of simple examples can show students the differences between the two cognate words. For instance, let's take the English word **parent**.

In Spanish, and also in French, there is a word that looks like the English word **parent**; yet the relationships which are represented are different. We can show the difference through example sentences like these:

> I have two parents. My mother is one of my parents.
> My father is my other parent. My sisters, brothers,
> aunts, and uncles are my relatives, but they are not my
> parents.

For a speaker of German, the English word **gymnasium** (among several other words) may require careful teaching because **gymnasium** in German means a school in which older children receive preparation for university study. In English, a gymnasium is a room or hall with apparatus for climbing, jumping, and various kinds of sports. To show the difference, we might use such example sentences as these:

> In an American school, the gymnasium has to be larger than the other rooms of the school because students from several classes sometimes meet there at the same time for physical exercise. There is usually a gymnasium in every school building, including elementary schools as well as secondary schools.

Skill in composing clear, simple example sentences is especially needed by teachers of Intermediate classes. Often there is an unexpected need for an example while the lesson is being taught. The teacher cannot spend class time thinking about the best way to explain the meaning of a word; an example must be offered immediately. Intermediate students need such help more than students at the Elementary level, where more of the vocabulary can be taught by pointing, or by using pictures, or by demonstrating an action.

MORE WORDS FOR COMMON AREAS OF LIVING

Like the Elementary student, the Intermediate student needs to learn words for common areas of living: words related to food, clothing, shelter, and so on. In classes for beginners, however, only a few words from each of these categories are taught. There is no attempt to teach all the English words for furniture (for instance)—or even all the most *important* words in the category of furniture. In Intermediate classes, on the other hand, there is a more systematic attempt to include the most commonly used words in various categories: categories like buildings, parts of a house, furniture, occupations, transportation, weather, health, and many more.

In the Intermediate textbook, words from several different categories are usually introduced together in each lesson. Perhaps they are presented in connection with a simple story; perhaps they are taught because the grammar part of the lesson requires them. To make vocabulary learning more systematic, therefore, the Intermediate student should keep a notebook. In the notebook there should be different sections for different categories of words— several pages reserved for weather words, other pages reserved for health words, and so on.

As words are presented in any lesson, the students should add each new word to the appropriate section of the notebook. Soon each student's notebook will have a useful list of words for buildings (**house**, **school**, **bank**, **post office**) and still other lists for words related to other areas of living. From time to time during the school year, the students should be given special opportunities to *use* this new vocabulary. We will now look at an activity that is designed to accomplish this.

An Activity for Learning Several Categories of Vocabulary

The class is divided into teams. Each team should consist of about four students. The teacher appoints a leader for each team and explains the next steps:

1. Each team will take responsibility for a different category of vocabulary. (The Furniture Team will be responsible for furniture words; the Food Team will be responsible for words like **meat**, **fish**, **butter**, etc.)

2. After each team has been given a category, it receives ten blank slips of paper. Each slip is to be used for one word from the team's category. Members of the team turn to the appropriate section in their notebooks and propose words for the slips. One member of the team carefully prints each of the chosen words on a separate slip, and the spellings are approved by all members of the team.

3. Slips from all the teams are placed in a box and thoroughly mixed by a student (with teacher supervision).

4. The teacher appoints a scorekeeper, who lists on the blackboard the names of the teams: Furniture, Food, Occupations, etc.

The scorekeeper will place a marker beside the name of any team that wins a point.

5. A time to stop the activity is stated.

6. Another student is asked to come to the front of the room and serve as announcer. The announcer draws a slip from the box, reads it aloud, and copies it on the blackboard. The class decides which category it fits. If it is a word for food, the scorekeeper places a mark beside Food on the blackboard. If some other team offers a good reason for also claiming that word—if, for instance, the word on the slip is **cook**, and the Occupations team can convince the class that **cook** belongs also in their category—*both* teams receive points.

7. The activity continues in the same way until the stated stopping time. The team with the most points at that time is the winner.

The slips which have been prepared by the teams should not be destroyed. They will have other uses, such as in a "category guessing game."

A Category Guessing Game
From time to time during the school year, there is instructional value in playing a *guessing game* that requires the use of English words. One such game is conducted as follows:

1. Four students are asked to come to the front of the classroom. One of them is selected to draw a slip from a box which contains words related to many different categories.

2. The student who has drawn the slip shows it to his three companions at the front of the room, but *not* to other members of the class.

3. The other members of the class try to guess the word on the slip which has been drawn from the box. They take turns asking first about the *category*, "Is it a word for food? For furniture? For transportation?" The four students who have seen the slip take

turns answering "No, it isn't" until the right category has been guessed.

4. After the correct category has been discovered (transportation, for instance) members of the class continue to ask Yes/No questions: "Is the word **bus**? Is it **taxi**? Is it **train**?"

5. The one whose guess is correct may draw a slip from the box the next time the game is played.

THE VALUE OF GAMES FOR VOCABULARY LEARNING

A number of chapters have suggested game-like activities for teaching vocabulary. One such activity has just been described.

In recommending games for vocabulary learning, the aim has *not* been to suggest pleasant ways of passing time. Time passes all too quickly in most classes, and the entertainment of students is not a teacher's responsibility. But language teachers *are* responsible for creating conditions which encourage vocabulary expansion, and a well-chosen game can help the students acquire English words.

Games are helpful because they can make students feel that certain words are important and necessary, because without those words, the object of the game cannot be achieved. Guessing games, for example, create conditions in which the use of the target language is necessary for leading the players to the correct guess. Here is a guessing game which encourages students to learn the English names for animals.

The Animal Game
1. Pictures of ten animals are displayed on the ledge of the blackboard. The teacher says, "We're going to play a guessing game and you will need to know the English names for these animals in order to play. Here is the name of each animal. Say it after me." Each name is written on the board after the students have said it. (Some farm animals like a goat, an ox, and a horse should be included, as well as zoo animals such as a monkey, a lion, an ele-

phant, and a giraffe. There should also be some animals found in
fields and woods, such as a rabbit and a mouse.)

2. For practice in the meaningful use of the animal names before
the game begins, the students are helped to observe and express
various facts about the animals which are displayed. For instance:

> Some of the animals are often found in a zoo. The ele-
> phant, lion, giraffe, and monkey are found in zoos.
> Others live on farms or in woods or fields. The ox and
> the goat are farm animals. The mouse sometimes lives
> in a field, but sometimes it lives in a house. The biggest
> of these animals is the elephant; the smallest is the
> mouse. The goat is bigger than a mouse but smaller
> than a horse.

3. The teacher announces that the game will now begin, and it
will be played as follows:

> "I'm going to think of one of these animals. You'll try
> to guess which one it is. First you must ask questions
> like, 'Does it live on a farm?' After you have discovered
> where it lives, then try to guess its size by asking 'Is it
> smaller than a horse?' and similar questions. Finally,
> when you think you can guess the name of the animal
> I'm thinking of, you may ask a question like, 'Is it a
> giraffe?' or 'Is it an ox?' All right. I'm thinking of one of
> these animals. Ask me some questions about it. I'll an-
> swer *only* when you ask me in *English*."

There are several things to notice about the game which has
just been described.

• When the students are told, "You will need to know the words
I'm about to give you in order to play a game," members of the
class who might not be attentive under other circumstances will
try very hard to learn the needed vocabulary.
• During the discussion that precedes the playing of the game, the
students are given help with the kinds of questions they will need
for success in their guessing. They are therefore more ready to try.

• By requiring the players to ask questions like, "Does it live in a zoo?" and "Is it smaller than a goat?" before asking directly, "Is it a rabbit?" we elicit a wider range of vocabulary, and we allow time for the slower students to become participants in the game.

• By warning the class, "I'll answer only when you ask me in English," the teacher avoids the necessity of constantly reminding students not to use their own language. If someone does so, the teacher just refuses to answer.

Not all games are helpful for language learning, of course. Board games like checkers cannot do much for vocabulary expansion because they do not require the players to speak *any* language during the game. Many games that involve physical activity are unsuitable, not only because they are too noisy for the classroom but because—in the excitement of the game—the players feel they must express their emotions in the native language.

Games which do not help students learn English do not belong in the English class. When we are considering possible games for use, we should ask, "Will this game help to make several English words seem interesting and important to my students?" That is a question to ask about anything we consider doing in class, including the use of pictures.

USING PICTURES IN THE INTERMEDIATE CLASS

In addition to game-like activities, there are other techniques for encouraging students to use English words while communicating information or ideas. Pictures (which have already been discussed in connection with vocabulary for beginners) can also be used at the Intermediate level in several helpful ways.

Pictures which show human situations (a child in a dentist's chair, an old couple on a bench in a park, several young people at the scene of an accident) often interest students at the Intermediate level. Students enjoy imagining who the pictured persons might be, where they are, what happened before the pictured moment, what might happen next.

A picture that suggests a story or a situation can be very valuable in the language class. In discussing such a picture, students will feel the *need* to learn English words for expressing their ideas; and we have already emphasized how desirable it is to make students feel words are needed.

There are, however, certain reasons why some teachers prefer not to engage the class in free discussion of a picture that stimulates students' imaginations. Teachers who are not native speakers of English sometimes avoid such discussions because they lack confidence in their ability to supply all the words the students might need for expressing their thoughts. Furthermore, even a teacher whose native language is English may prefer not to invite free discussion for the following reason: very often only two or three eager members of the class actually participate, while the rest pay little attention to what is being said.

We can avoid the difficulties that may arise from using interesting pictures for class discussion if we ask students to *write* about the situations which the pictures represent. A few of the better students may be invited to write about a picture while the other members of the class are doing less advanced work with the teacher.

The more imaginative students enjoy *stretching* their English while writing stories. It is good for them to try new uses for the English they have been learning. Naturally, the stories they write will contain many errors. But when the papers are handed in, we should not worry about those errors and we should not make the writer feel ashamed of them. Most of the mistakes should be ignored. A few suggestions will be helpful to the writer; but mainly we should just show interest in the story and praise the writer's attempts to use English words. Even if the writing is far from perfect, the student will have learned vocabulary through his efforts to communicate. There will be other activities designed to produce correct sentences. In those activities we can improve students' grammar, punctuation, and other language skills. When students are invited to stretch their English, to do as well as they can with what they already know, we should permit them to write without constant fear of making mistakes.

At the Intermediate level of instruction, students should be given many opportunities to *try* to communicate in English, even when their efforts lead them to make errors in language use. Unlike beginners, Intermediate students know enough English to experiment with ways of expressing their ideas in the target language. They should be encouraged to do so.

In this chapter we have described activities that require Intermediate students to use English for communication. We have noted that learners at this level can understand definitions that make use of English words which have already been taught. We have stressed the importance of example sentences, such as those found in learner's dictionaries that have been specially prepared for students of ESL.

This chapter has drawn attention to the *kinds* of words to be learned at the Intermediate level. Like beginners, Intermediate students need words pertaining to common areas of living. In contrast to beginners, however, Intermediate students should make a more *systematic* study of those life-areas and categories.

We have considered in this chapter the value of notebooks in which students keep separate sections for various categories of vocabulary. This recording of words by categories has a practical function, which becomes clear when we engage the students in activities that require the use of words from various categories. (Such activities include contests and games. As we have noted, however, game-like activities belong in the classroom only when they help the students master the language.)

In addition, this chapter has called attention to something which is more true of Intermediate students than of those in Elementary classes. It is the fact that certain activities which are suitable for some members of the class are not helpful to others. (The writing of imaginative stories in response to pictures is such an activity.) The next chapter will say more about techniques that serve the various kinds of students often found within one Intermediate class.

·ACTIVITIES·

1. Using English vocabulary that Intermediate students already know, write simple definitions for each of the following words: **kitten**, **damp**, **purple**.

2. If a learner's dictionary (like the *Oxford Student's Dictionary of American English* or the *Longman Dictionary of Contemporary English*) is available, find the definitions of **kitten**, **damp**, and **purple** in that dictionary. Compare your definitions with those you have found in a standard dictionary intended for native English-speakers.

3. For each of the words in the following list, write an illustrative sentence that could show your students the kind of life situation in which someone might experience the emotion named by that word. *Examples:*

  • He was filled with **anger** when his son refused to obey.
  • He was filled with **delight** when he heard the wonderful news.

1. anger   4. fear   7. pride
2. delight   5. grief   8. relief
3. disappointment   6. pity   9. shame

4. Suppose you are planning to engage your students in a contest. It is a contest to be won by the team that can give the most words belonging to a certain category within a limited time, without looking at the lists in their notebooks. Describe how you would prepare students for this activity, and write the directions which you would give them for conducting the contest.

5. Think of a game that many people know and enjoy playing. Explain how you could adapt it for use in teaching English vocabulary.

6. The picture below could be used by the more imaginative members of an Intermediate class for the writing of a story. Imagine you are a student in that class. Write a story such as the one that the student might write.

7. In a book or a magazine, find some other picture that might encourage students in the class to write a story. (If you cannot find a good picture, write a description of a picture that an artist could make for your English class.)

·CHAPTER SIX·
DIFFERENCES AMONG INTERMEDIATE STUDENTS

In Chapter 5 we considered the value of assigning to a few of the better students a task which might not be suitable for slower learners in the class. We also noted the value of dividing the class into teams.

Dividing a class into smaller work groups is an important technique at the Intermediate and Advanced levels of English instruction. It is less possible at the Elementary level, because beginners do not yet have enough English to enable them to work together in groups without the constant presence of a teacher. Besides, in a class for beginners all students are likely to need the same kind of work. In the Intermediate class, however, there are usually a few students who know more than their classmates—and sometimes a few others who know much less than most members of the class. For that reason, Intermediate classes benefit from small-group work. Some groups can then be given simpler tasks, while others do tasks that move them ahead as quickly as possible.

Many teachers who agree that group work is desirable have very little time for preparing material to be used by groups. Such teachers may wish to try some of the following activities, which require no preparation (except to give a copy of the directions to the leader of the group—a group usually consisting of three or four students).

TASKS FOR SMALL GROUPS
(OR FOR INDIVIDUAL STUDENTS)

TASK 1:

Using the category sections of your notebooks, make a list of 20 pairs of words that belong together. Each member of the pair should be from a *different* category. For instance, one pair might be **hat** (from the Clothing category) and **head** (from your list of parts of the body). When your list is complete, show it to the teacher.

TASK 2:

Using the category sections of your notebooks, make lists of

4 farm animals
4 zoo animals
4 things that have four legs
4 things that are made of glass
4 things that are made of wood

TASK 3:

Here are ten sets of words. In each set there is one word that does not belong in that set. Find it and write a sentence that tells why it is different. (*After* each member of your group has done this, compare your answers with those of the other members of your group.)

1. book   magazine   lettuce
(Lettuce is different, because people don't read it.)
2. coffee   rice   tea
(_____ is different, because people don't _____ it.)
3. paper   tennis   soccer
4. meat   fish   money
5. beans   hats   shirts
6. airplanes   buses   scissors
7. monkeys   ladders   steps
8. floors   rugs   flowers
9. horses   rings   watches
10. bread   rubber   cake

TASK 4:

Here are eight English words for things. Write a sentence about the most common or ordinary use of each thing. Then list three other *possible* uses.

1. spoon
We use a spoon for eating. Other possible uses for a spoon are (1) digging a hole, (2) carrying an egg from the stove to the sink, and (3) taking a fly out of a bowl of soup.

2. pencil	5. pillow	7. coat hanger
3. nail file	6. toothbrush	8. clothesline
4. tablecloth		

TASK 5:

During the first five minutes of this activity, each member of your group should write answers (in English) to the following questions, expressing his or her own opinion:

1. What are some of the things that cause trouble between parents and teenagers today?
2. What are some characteristics of the *best* parents? (What do they do? What don't they do?)

After five minutes, exchange papers with other members of your group. How many of the answers are similar? How many are different?

It can be seen that some of these tasks are easier than others. (For example, 4 and 5 require more English than 1 and 2.) Thus the quicker students may be working on more difficult exercises while the slower ones are engaged in simpler tasks.

Teachers who have used these activities for group work have made the following suggestion: After each task has been completed, and the teacher has seen the group's papers, some of the results should be shared with the rest of the class. For instance, the group that worked on Task 5 might report which answers were given by most members of the group. Some of the sentences which were prepared for Task 4 should be copied on the board, or on a large sheet of paper, to be displayed to the class.

GROUP ACTIVITIES USING PICTURES

Several activities involving the use of pictures have already been described. Most of them are suitable for small-group work as well as for use with the entire class. Two additional uses of pictures with small groups will now be suggested.

When available, a copy of the *Oxford Picture Dictionary of American English*[1] can be used by three students, working together as follows:

1. The three students choose a page that looks interesting. (Let's say they have chosen page 36, which shows a scene on a farm. On the dictionary page, various parts of the scene are numbered; each number refers to an English word at the bottom of the page.)

2. After looking together at the scene, the group chooses *twelve* of the pictured animals, persons, and things that especially interest them. Each member of the group takes responsibility for learning the English names for *four* of those selected parts of the scene. (One student may choose to learn the English names for the pictured fence, bull, saddle, and tractor. Each of the other group members will learn four other English names for other parts of the scene.)

3. At the end of five minutes, each group member teaches "his" English words to the other two members of the group.

4. All twelve English words are then listed by the group, and the list is given to the teacher.

If a picture dictionary is not available, pictures from magazines may be used, as follows:

1. Before class, the teacher selects three or four pictures, each showing a different scene. One, for example, may be an office scene with a typewriter, photocopier, telephone, file, wastepaper basket, and so on.

2. After mounting each pictured scene on a sheet of cardboard,

[1]E. C. Parnwell, *Oxford Picture Dictionary of American English* (New York: Oxford University Press, 1978), p. 36.

the teacher prints a number on every object for which an English name should be learned, then lists all those names below the picture, each with its number.

3. During the group work period, all the pictures are given to a group of three students. Each member of the group chooses a different picture, learns the English names for the objects which are pictured in that scene, then teaches those words to the other members of the group.

One advantage of having students teach words to other students is that it gives the individual learner a *personal interest* in certain English words. Another advantage is that weaker students are induced to participate, because each student is the sole possessor of needed pieces of information. It is well known that we learn something best when we have to teach it. For that reason, language students need opportunities to teach others, even when a few words are all that can be taught.

USING EXERCISES FROM THE TEXTBOOK FOR GROUP WORK

For many group activities, no set of "correct" answers can be provided in advance. However, there are other tasks for which a set of expected answers can be supplied. A card that shows the expected answers can be given to the group leader, who is responsible for making sure that members of the group know what the answers are.

It is often possible to divide a class into teams of three or four students for work on certain vocabulary exercises that are found in the textbook lessons. Here is such an exercise, from *A Reading Spectrum*, Book 5 of the Progressive Reading Series.[2]

EXERCISE D.
Give the noun form of each of the following adjectives:
    Example: different—difference

---

[2]*A Reading Spectrum, Book 5,* Progressive Reading Series (Washington, D.C.: United States Information Agency, 1975), p. 49.

1. deep	3. hot	5. long
2. high	4. wide	6. strong

When such an exercise is used for group work, the teacher asks one member of the small group to serve as leader. The leader's job is to make sure that each member takes a turn at giving an answer; and if that member's answer is wrong, the leader corrects it, reading from the card of answers which the teacher has prepared. For *Exercise D*, the leader's card would read:

1. depth	3. heat	5. length
2. height	4. width	6. strength

The experience of "teaching" the group is helpful to the leader. Another advantage is that each of the two or three others in the group has more than one chance to answer. That is not possible when the exercise is used with the entire class.

In many textbooks there are *scrambled sentence* exercises. Although these are generally intended for practice in reading or writing, they also contribute to vocabulary expansion because students must know (or learn) the meanings of words in the sentences before they can put the sentences in proper order. For instance, a student who has not already learned the word **towel** will learn it while rearranging the following scrambled sentences:

He used warm water and soap.
Anwar washed his hair last night.
Then he dried his hair with a big white towel.

Scrambled sentence exercises can be done by a group of three students, working together, while other members of the class are engaged in other tasks. The group receives a large card with instructions, as follows:

In each of the following sets, there are three sentences that tell what William did yesterday. Each sentence is correct, but the sentences are not in the right order. In Set 1, for example, Sentence (b) should come first, because William got up before he ate breakfast; and after that, he went to school. Put the sentences of each set in the right order, and then copy them.

SET 1

(a) He went to school.

(b) He got up.

(c) He ate breakfast.

SET 2

(a) He said goodbye to his friend.

(b) He had a conversation with his friend.

(c) He said hello to his friend.

SET 3

(a) He bought film for his camera.

(b) He took a picture of the football team.

(c) He put film into his camera.

SET 4

(a) He ran to the river.

(b) He swam to the other side of the river.

(c) He jumped into the river.

SET 5

(a) He went to bed.

(b) He took a shower.

(c) He took off his clothes.

When such an exercise is used by a small group (instead of by the entire class) the three members of the group must agree on the correct order. Then one of the three writes the sentences (as dictated by the others). When the task is completed, the group members take the paper to the teacher, who checks the sentences.

Many of the exercises which are found in textbooks have certain expected answers, which can be put on cards for the use of the group leader. The following show two common types of textbook exercises, with the answers that should be provided on cards for the group leaders:

TYPE 1:
True–False Exercises
Example:
1. A lion is a large animal.
2. Mice are larger than rabbits.

Answers
1. True
2. False

TYPE 2:
Multiple Choice Exercises
Example: *Answers*
1. Mirrors are made of   1. (c)
(a) milk   (b) wine   (c) glass

Usually, in most language programs, such an exercise in the textbook is done by the entire class. The teacher asks a student to answer the first question, another student is chosen to answer the second, and so on—until each member of the class has taken a turn. Occasionally, however, it is a good idea to vary this procedure by assigning the exercise to small groups. When the teacher gives clear directions, and moves from group to group for supervision of the activities, the small-group use of textbook exercises is valuable in at least three ways.

1. Each student has more opportunities to use the new vocabulary than in the conventional use of the same exercise by the entire class.

2. The student who serves as leader will benefit from the experience of correcting his classmates' answers through the use of the answer card which the teacher has prepared. (In effect, he has to pay attention to *all* the questions and to know all the answers—not just one.)

3. The occasional use of such group work increases the students' interest in English and keeps their minds alert.

KEEPING THE INTERMEDIATE STUDENT INTERESTED AND ENCOURAGED

Keeping the students' minds alert is a particular problem in many Intermediate classes. Teachers often mention the need to increase the Intermediate students' interest. A beginning student is usually somewhat interested; the experience of learning the language is new enough so that he is pleased to be able to say and understand a few foreign words. When students reach the Intermediate level, however, the experience is no longer new. Furthermore, the students have become aware of the difficulties. Their efforts may bring less satisfaction, fewer rewards.

When students come to the Intermediate class in a discouraged state of mind, they need activities which offer immediate rewards for making an effort to learn. One of the best rewards is the satisfaction of being able to *do* something by means of the English words that one knows. That is one of the principal reasons for using simplified readings at the Intermediate level of instruction.

Simplified readings create a helpful sense of achievement. The student feels encouraged by being able to read a story or essay in English without great difficulty.

There are several other things that an Intermediate student can *do* as a result of having learned certain English words. One of the most rewarding is the crossword puzzle which has been specially prepared for learners of ESL. (Those intended for native speakers are generally too difficult for Intermediate students. They require a knowledge of many words that students rarely learn in school.) When a student succeeds in completing a puzzle, his success shows him that he is making progress after all: he is able to *use* the vocabulary he has learned. ("An Introductory Crossword Puzzle" appears in Appendix E.)

As earlier chapters have pointed out, there is another helpful way to give students experience in the use of English words. Students may be asked to respond to commands which are given in English. At the Intermediate level, the commands can (and should) make use of more complex grammatical structures, as well as more advanced vocabulary. For instance, after easy commands like **stand up** and **sit down** have been reviewed, students may be asked to perform actions in response to such commands as the following:

- When I stop clapping my hands, turn your head to the right.
- Put both hands on your shoulders without turning your head.
- Raise your right hand if Europe is a country, but touch your shoulder if it's a continent.

Each command may be spoken by the teacher; or a student who reads well may be asked to read the command aloud from a card which the teacher has prepared. Before the class as a whole responds, the action may be demonstrated by one or two of the better students, seated at the front of the classroom with their backs to the class.

When such an exercise is used during the first five minutes of the class period, it can help to focus students' attention on English. But it may be even more helpful in the middle of the class hour, or toward the end of a lesson which some students have found discouragingly difficult. Discouragement can be reduced when the students find themselves able to *use* English for responding to (or giving) complex commands.

English for the Outside World

At the Intermediate level, students also need to see how their growing knowledge of English is preparing them for situations beyond the classroom. The following technique is intended to have that effect, in classes where English is a *foreign* language— where some language other than English is the community's chief means of communication. In such a class, there is value in class discussions related to practical situations which are described to the students as follows:

Imagine that we have some English-speaking friends, a family from the United States. We'll call them the

Halls. The Halls are visiting our town, but they don't know the language that is used here. They have asked our help with several problems. Where shall we take them for help with each problem?

1. Mr. Hall has a toothache.
2. Mrs. Hall wants to buy material for a dress, and then she will need to find someone to make the dress for her.
3. The Halls' daughter, Sandra (a teenager), can't use her hairdryer because their hotel doesn't have the right kind of electrical current.
4. The Halls' son, Eddie (10 years old), doesn't like foreign food. His parents have promised him something like a hamburger.

After these and other problems have been discussed, selected students may be asked to construct dialogs. In each dialog, someone in the class is talking with a member of the Hall family about arrangements—when and where they will meet to obtain the desired object or service.

If English is being learned in the United States, the exercise will take a different form, but the purpose will be the same: to put the students' growing vocabulary to practical use. The class may be told:

Imagine that a family (we'll call them the X family) have just arrived from another country. They plan to live here. Since you know more English than they do, they have asked you to help them. First we'll list on the board several kinds of help the family will need. (The students will know—better than the teacher—what kinds of help the new family will need.) Then we'll use the yellow pages of the telephone directory to decide where we should take the X family for things and services they need.

In both these activities, students are led to consider *problems* which they might help people solve through their knowledge of English. Both activities also illustrate an important point about Intermediate classes. The point is this: In Intermediate classes, we make a special effort to introduce vocabulary that is *related to the lives of English-speaking people*. It is usually at the Intermediate level that we teach words like **hamburger** and **hairdryer** (even when hamburgers and hairdryers are not part of our students' everyday lives).

As Chapter 2 pointed out, vocabulary for the Elementary level of instruction consists mainly of words for persons and things in the classroom, in the students' homes, in the local community. At the Intermediate level, however, we begin to go beyond the students' immediate experience. We teach **snow** and **subway**, for instance, even where neither snow nor subways are found. Techniques for teaching words that have special meanings among native speakers of English will be described in the next chapter.

·ACTIVITIES·

1. Describe a task for *small groups* of students in the Intermediate class (similar to Task 2 on page 60).

2. Add five more sets of words to the ten sets which are listed in Task 3 on page 60. (You will probably find suitable words for this activity in the textbooks which are used in your own classes. Another possible source is the list of "Useful Nouns and Verbs" in Appendix C, page 121.)

3. Suggest some other activity (*not* described in this chapter) that could be done by a small group of students who are more advanced than their Intermediate classmates. Write the directions that you could give to the leader of that group.

4. In a textbook intended for Intermediate students, find a vocabulary exercise which could be used by small groups. Prepare an answer card for the group leader.

5. Write three sets of scrambled sentences like the sets on page 65. Ask a friend to put the sentences in proper order. See if your friend's rearrangement is the order you intended.

6. Write a series of commands containing Intermediate-level vocabulary and grammatical structures (as complex as the commands on page 68).

7. Mention problems which the class might discuss in relation to helping families (like the problems of the Hall family and the X family in this chapter).

·CHAPTER SEVEN·
NEW KINDS OF MEANINGS FOR INTERMEDIATE CLASSES

Chapters 5 and 6 have drawn attention to several special characteristics of Intermediate students:

1. They need to extend their knowledge of vocabulary related to common areas of experience (food, clothing, transportation, health, human relations).

2. They have already learned many of the basic words, so the teacher can (and should) use simple English explanations for introducing new vocabulary.

3. Some Intermediate students have learned more English than other members of the same class; therefore, different activities for individuals and small groups should frequently be arranged. (Techniques for doing this have been suggested.)

4. Intermediate students have reached a point in their language study where many become discouraged and lose interest. (Techniques for dealing with this problem have been described.)

5. One reason for the Intermediate student's possible discouragement is the increasing difficulty of the vocabulary which must be learned—especially vocabulary related to the lives of people for whom English is the native language.

English is sometimes used when no native speaker is present. A Japanese businessman may speak English with a Brazilian, for instance. Nevertheless, a major goal of most students is to understand English as it is used among native speakers. Learners hope to be able to read books and magazines intended for native speakers. They also want to understand the radio and TV programs that native speakers listen to.

Those who write textbooks for Intermediate classes generally keep that fact in mind. Vocabulary lessons—and reading selections—introduce words like **picnic**, **sandwich**, **supermarket**, **car pool**, **baby sitter**, and many others that represent common features of life in English-speaking countries.

If the customs represented by such English words are not part of life on the local scene, such vocabulary may be hard to understand. On the other hand, the English words may have a special appeal if they represent new experiences that are becoming part of the students' own lives. (We noted in Chapter 2 how easily an expression like **rock star** is learned when it stands for a new idea for which the students' language has no special name.)

Textbooks generally provide help in teaching words for special aspects of life among native speakers of English. Modern textbooks contain short readings (in simplified English) that deal with common life situations. The most helpful readings are very short stories that show what people do and think and say in those situations. The teacher's job then is to encourage students to *think* about the reading selection. If the story introduces the term **baby sitter**, for instance, we ask, "Why did the family need a baby sitter?" "Was the baby sitter really a servant?" "What part of the story shows us the age and economic status of the baby sitter?" "How do we know that baby sitters are treated like guests in some ways?"

In addition to acquiring such *new* vocabulary words, Intermediate students need also to learn new meanings for many of the English words they already know. In particular, they need to become aware of what those common words mean to native speakers of English.

WHAT COMMON ENGLISH WORDS MEAN TO NATIVE SPEAKERS

Let's consider a few of the English words our Intermediate students already know: words like **family**, **breakfast**, and **kitchen**.

When we say that the students know the word **family**, we mean that they have associated it with a word in their own language, the word that corresponds most closely to the English word **family**. They assume that **family** means to a speaker of English what the corresponding word in their language means to them. But very often there are differences.

In many languages, the word for **family** regularly represents several related persons—uncles, aunts, cousins, and grand-parents, as well as father and mother and their children. But this is not the group that English-speaking Mr. A has in mind when he says, "I wish I could spend more time with my **family**." (He means "with my wife and our children.") The other relatives—in most cases—do not live with Mr. and Mrs. A. Perhaps they live hundreds of miles away. This knowledge is needed for any real understanding of the English word **family**. Without it, one does not get the full meaning of a sentence like "The American family has many problems today."

The word **breakfast**, too, is only partly learned when students know it represents the first meal of the day. To develop anything like full understanding of **breakfast**, one must get answers to such questions as these:

- What kinds of food and drink are (and are not) commonly found on the breakfast table?
- How early in the day do people generally eat breakfast? How late in the day?
- How common is it to start the day without any breakfast at all?
- In which age group is breakfast most often omitted?

The answers to such questions are not in dictionaries. Yet they help to form the meanings that the word **breakfast** has for speakers of English.

In the same way, we could ask questions that would help to reveal the English-speaking person's meanings for **kitchen**—the _social_ meanings that are not supplied by a dictionary. One cannot _find_ full meanings for any word, even in dictionaries for learners of

ESL. One such dictionary (*Oxford Advanced Learner's Dictionary of Current English*) does include a helpful fact about kitchens that is seldom found elsewhere. In addition to stating that a kitchen is a room in which meals are prepared, it indicates that in many homes the kitchen is a general purpose room where (for example) meals are eaten by the family.[3]

No dictionary, however, has space for all the facts that make the word **kitchen** mean what it means to native speakers. There is not space enough to explain that

• even in a family with three cars, members of the family may spend a great deal of time in their kitchen;
• such a family probably has no servant, so the kitchen work is done by members of the family (including the husband);
• the kitchen is therefore one of the finest rooms in the house, with a stove, refrigerator, dishwasher, and other appliances which are newer and more expensive than the furniture of the living room.

All of these facts, and more, contribute to the social meanings of **kitchen**.

How to Help Students Learn Social Meanings
It is hard for students to learn the social meanings of words like **family**, **breakfast**, and **kitchen**. It is especially difficult when English is being studied in a country where it is not the language of daily life. But teachers can help, even if English is not their native language.

We can help, first, by making students aware that social meanings exist. We can also help by drawing students' attention to the special meanings that are revealed in stories and other readings about English-speaking people.

Here, for instance, is a paragraph that reveals some of the meanings of the word **school**. It shows what may be expected to happen in a classroom in an English-speaking country; it shows what a teacher may be expected to do and *not do*; it shows that

[3]A.S. Hornby, *Oxford Advanced Learner's Dictionary of Current English*, 3d ed, (Oxford: Oxford University Press, 1974), p. 466.

people are not surprised when classes are conducted in that way. All of this is part of the meaning that native speakers of English attach to the word **school**:

> Some eighteen year old students are having a discussion lesson. There is a teacher there but he refuses to say very much. He never interrupts even when a student is saying something rather stupid. Occasionally he asks a few questions; that is all.[4]

Suppose the word for **school** in the students' language represents a place where discussions are not considered a proper part of a lesson, where teachers are expected to talk much more than students, where students who say something stupid should be interrupted immediately. In that case, the social meanings of the English word **school** should be noted. Students' attention should be drawn to them through such questions as these:

1. What does this story tell us about discussions among students in English-speaking schools?
2. In those schools, are students expected to talk much?
3. Why doesn't the teacher in this story correct students when they say something stupid?
4. What seems to be the main purpose of such a class? (Is the main purpose to give students information?)

Through such questions, we can call attention to the ideas, feelings, and customs that combine to form part of the meaning of a common English word—a word that may have a somewhat different meaning in the students' own experience.

It is mainly through stories that students learn what certain phrases mean to speakers of English in the United States: **in the west** and **from the south**, for instance. (Other languages have words for **north, south, east,** and **west**; but those terms represent ideas and feelings quite different from the social meanings associated with the American English words.)

[4]R. O'Neill and others, *English in Situations* (Oxford: Oxford University Press, 1970), p. 168.

Learning Social Meanings from Native Speakers

Stories can help us teach social meanings because a story provides a kind of indirect contact with native speakers of the language. Of course, *direct* contact with native speakers can be even more helpful. Where English is not the language of the community, it may not be easy for students to meet English-speaking people. Even there, however, occasionally an English-speaking visitor can spend a few minutes in the ESL classroom. Furthermore, the class may have a pen pal with whom letters are exchanged.

Unfortunately, such opportunities for communication are often wasted because students do not know how to use them. They do not know what information could be gained, or how to phrase questions for obtaining it.

Here are a few of the many questions ESL students might usefully ask in letters to pen pals—or in conversations with young persons whose native language is English:

1. How far is your school from your home? How do you get there?

2. Do students in your school wear uniforms? If not, what do you generally wear to school?

3. How many hours do you spend on homework every day?

4. Do you live in a house or an apartment? In the city or the country or a small town?

5. How many people live in your home? Are they all related to you? Where do your grandparents live?

6. Do teenagers in your family ever disagree with the adults? What do they argue about?

7. Who prepares the meals in your family? Who washes the dishes?

8. What kinds of food do you like best? What kinds don't you like?

9. Who talks most at mealtime? What do members of the family talk about at meals? In which room do you most often eat?

10. If a teenager in the family disobeys the adults, what happens? How were you punished when you were a young child?

These are only a few of the questions that could lead toward understanding of common words like **school**, **home**, **family**, and **food** in relation to English-speaking life. (Additional questions are listed in Appendix D.) Answers to some of them can be found in the stories, dialogs, and readings that modern textbooks provide for Intermediate students. Answers can also be obtained through correspondence and conversations with native speakers, when full use is made of such opportunities.

Learning word meanings is a lifetime job, even for native speakers. From every experience we gain more understanding. When direct experience with speakers of the language cannot be arranged, much can still be learned from the indirect experience that stories provide.

As teachers, we can help students notice what certain words mean to speakers of English. That is one of the special aims of the Intermediate vocabulary class. Other objectives include the following:

• Show students how much they are able to do with the words they have already learned.
• Enable the better students to progress more rapidly (by providing special tasks for individuals and groups).

When these aims are accomplished, students are prepared for the Advanced stage of English instruction. Techniques for Advanced classes will be suggested in the next chapter.

·ACTIVITIES·

1. Here is a dialog that appears in a reader for Intermediate students:[5]

SUMMER JOBS

DAN: It's almost vacation time. Have you found a summer job yet?

JOE: I suppose I can work at the boys' camp where I worked last summer. But camp jobs don't pay much.

DAN: I think I can get a job at the Edgewater Hotel. A friend of mine was a waiter there last summer. The pay wasn't good, but he got lots of tips.

JOE: My sister worked there last summer, making beds and cleaning bathrooms. She didn't like it, but she earned quite a lot of money.

DAN: A friend of my sister's did that one summer.

JOE: What I want is a job outside. After sitting in college classes all winter, I'd like a job in the open air.

DAN: The high school kids earn a lot of money every summer cutting grass. My brother is only fourteen but he gets five dollars every time he cuts

[5]*A Reading Sampler*, *Book 3*, Progressive Reading Series
(Washington, D.C.: U.S. Information Agency, 1975), p. 54.

somebody's grass, and it only takes him an hour.
He just rides around on the machine that he
bought and the machine does all the work.

JOE: That's pretty good. I used to cut grass when I
was in high school. But now I thought I might
work for a road-building company, or something
like that.

DAN: It would be good experience. You could earn a
lot, too.

From such a dialog, students can learn some of the social
meanings of a word like **vacation**. (For instance: To a native
speaker of English, a middle-class student's **vacation** often means
a time for working—in a hotel, at a summer camp, or as a gar-
dener or builder of roads.) What social meanings are suggested
here for the words **job**, **student**, **waiter**, **machine**, and **experience**?

2. Ask three people from the same English-speaking country
what they usually eat for lunch. Are there any kinds of food that
are mentioned by all three people? Compare their understanding
of **lunch** with your students' understanding of that word.

3. To show your students what social meanings may be attached
to a commonly used word like **cat**, help the students find out how
native speakers of English would answer the following questions:

1. Does a cat usually live outside, or inside someone's
house?
2. Does a cat ever sleep on its owner's bed?
3. What do cats eat? (Do their owners ever buy special
food for them?)
4. Do some people buy toys for their cats?
5. If a cat becomes sick, does its owner ever take it to a
doctor?

4. Discuss the answers to the questions about cats. Consider how the answers might help your students understand what a native speaker of English might really mean by a sentence like: "I have three cats." How do the social meanings of **cat** compare to the meanings of the corresponding word in your students' language?

5. The words and phrases listed below should be understood by students who have completed basic courses in English as a Second Language. Each item in the list refers to something very common in the experience of people living in the United States. Which of the items (if any) would need to be explained to your class because the students' own life experience has not prepared them to understand those vocabulary items?

1. Halloween costumes   6. a three-story house
2. jack-o'-lanterns   7. floor wax
3. trick or treat   8. a laundromat
4. a front lawn   9. a rare steak
5. a shingled roof   10. a Thanksgiving turkey

6. Examine the textbooks which are used in your own ESL program. Which words and phrases in those books refer to areas of experience with which your students are not personally acquainted?

·CHAPTER EIGHT·
TEACHING VOCABULARY IN ADVANCED CLASSES

In Advanced classes, we have two major aims. One is to prepare students for the kind of English used by and for native speakers. (For this reason, there is less use of simplified material which is made easy for the learner; there is more use of material intended for speakers of English.) The other special aim is to help students become independent, responsible for their own learning.

Advanced students are almost at the end of the language program. If learning is to continue beyond the end of the course, the students will have to depend on their own efforts and habits of study. Dictionaries therefore become especially important. Advanced students must be taught to use them well.

As the material which is read becomes increasingly difficult, there are many more new words to be explained. The teacher cannot—and should not—help students learn all of them. When the teacher spends an entire class period explaining vocabulary—writing words and their meanings on the blackboard—there are three unfortunate results: (1) the students remain too dependent on the teacher; (2) opportunities for learning to use a dictionary are lost; and (3) no class time is left for the *communicative use* of the language. How then can we help students understand the many new words they meet? And what should they be taught about the use of dictionaries?

DICTIONARIES AS PASSPORTS TO INDEPENDENCE

When we speak of dictionaries for English as a Second Language, it is realistic to assume that the one most commonly used is the two-language dictionary. Students naturally turn first to dictionaries which define English words in their mother tongue. Although bilingual dictionaries are unsatisfactory in *many* ways, they are less expensive than all-English dictionaries and more easily obtained.

It does no harm to start with a bilingual dictionary, *if* the students are taught to use it properly and if they are soon taught how to obtain more accurate meanings from an all-English dictionary.

Any dictionary can serve to introduce a number of points about dictionary use. First, *before* opening the dictionary, students should follow these steps:

1. Think carefully about the *entire sentence* in which the unfamiliar word appears. Ask yourself: How much of the sentence can I understand even without knowing that word?

2. Look carefully at the unknown word. What *kind* of word is it? A noun? A verb? An adjective?

3. Think of some *possible* meanings for that kind of word in that sentence. If the word is a noun, might it name some *thing*? Some person? Some idea? Does it probably represent something good? Something bad?

When the student thinks carefully about the whole sentence before looking in his dictionary, he may find that he really does not *need* to look up the unknown word. Suppose, for instance, that the student does not know the word **reward** in this sentence: "One of the **rewards** that space travelers receive is the beautiful view of the planet on which we live."

A student who has been taught to think about the whole sentence will say to himself, "I know that **rewards** is a noun here, because it is used after **the**. The sentence tells me a reward is something that is **received**; and it must be something good, because the beautiful view is called a reward."

This kind of thinking may produce enough understanding of the word **reward** for the student's present purpose. More exact understanding can come later, when the word is met again—as it will be, if it is essential or commonly used.

But if the student does decide he should confirm his impression by looking up **reward** in his dictionary, he is now better able to choose from among possible meanings. Having thought about the entire sentence, he can choose more intelligently from among the meanings offered by the dictionary.

There is another reason why students should be taught to think about the sentence before looking up a word. Suppose the word **equipped** is unfamiliar to someone reading this sentence: "Weather stations are **equipped** to receive direct reports from U.S. weather satellites."

If the student looks for **equipped** in his dictionary, he probably will not be able to find it. However, the word **equip** is quite sure to be there. Those who have looked carefully at the sentence will have guessed that **equipped** is the **-ed** form of a verb and that the verb probably ends in a single **p**. Now the student is ready to look for **equip** and to find out whether the verb means something like **establish**, **permit**, or **require**—or something different from any of these. With such a question in mind, a student can make wise choices among the listed possibilities.

Thus far we have stressed the need for careful thought before opening the dictionary. Imagine now that the dictionary is open. Some students may still need help in reaching the part of the dictionary where the needed definition appears. For some, the simple task of finding the right page may require instruction and practice. (This is especially difficult for students whose language uses a different alphabet and also for those with little experience in the use of reference materials.)

When finding the needed word is a problem, we show the class how to use the key words at the top of each page. We assign such tasks as these:

1. Give the number of the page where each of the following is defined: **fog, loaf, lope, roly-poly**

2. Arrange the following words in alphabetical order:
slump, sluggish, shadow, sloppy, slope, spate

Careful thought is also required *after* the possible meanings
have been found. Working together, students and teacher should
consider the possible definitions, discussing their appropriateness
to the sentence and the paragraph where the word has appeared.
Such a discussion takes time, but it is often a necessary part of the
students' training.

When many words need to be looked up, it is often possible
to divide the work among several students. Two members of the
class may take responsibility for the difficult words in one paragraph, while other paragraphs are assigned to different pairs of
students. Each team is instructed to list the unfamiliar words in
the team's paragraph and to think about the sentence in which
each of those words appears. Team members next decide which
meaning in their dictionary best fits the context. After working in
this way for a few minutes, the teams come together to share their
findings, with approval or corrections by the teacher.

This sort of activity helps the students develop initiative and
responsibility. When just two students are held responsible for
"teaching" certain words to their classmates, the words become
important to them. Sharing the responsibility with a partner encourages careful selection of meanings from those offered by the
dictionary. The report to the class gives the teacher a chance to see
how efficiently the individual students are using their dictionaries.

What if the bilingual dictionary offers *no* meaning that seems
right for the word in that sentence? This often happens. Many
small two-language dictionaries give only one or two meanings for
any English word. When there is no helpful definition to be found
in the dictionary used by the students, an important fact has been
made clear: some dictionaries are very poor; certain dictionaries
are much more helpful than others.

Special Learner's Dictionaries

The best dictionaries for English as a Second Language are
learner's dictionaries, such as the *Oxford Student's Dictionary of*

American English and the *Longman Dictionary of Contemporary English*. Both contain much valuable information in addition to their helpful definitions of words. There should be at least one copy of a learner's dictionary in every English classroom, and students should be encouraged to use it.

To show students the advantage of such a dictionary, we can compare the help it offers to the meanings found in bilingual dictionaries. Here, for instance, is some of the information students can find in the *Longman Dictionary of Contemporary English* when they look up the word **reward**. Two possible definitions are given, including "something gained as return for work or service."[6] To illustrate this meaning, the dictionary gives the following sentence: "He will expect some reward after working so hard."

Example sentences (which generally are found only in all-English dictionaries) often do more than definitions to make the meaning clear. In addition, an example sentence often has another advantage for learners of English. It shows which word or words usually accompany the word which the student has looked up. For instance, the following sentences illustrate the use of **depend** (in the Oxford dictionary):

Children depend on their parents for food and clothing.
You can always depend upon John to be there when he
is needed.[7]

These sentences show that **depend** is often accompanied by **on** or **upon**.

When a learner's dictionary is available for students' use, we can give students a list of verbs or adjectives, along with the following instructions:

1. In the dictionary, find an example sentence for each verb or adjective on this list.
2. Copy each example sentence.
3. Draw a line below the *preposition* which is used with the verb or adjective that the sentence illustrates.

[6]*Longman Dictionary of Contemporary English* (London: Longman, 1978), p. 951.

[7]A.S. Hornby, *Oxford Student's Dictionary of American English* (Oxford: Oxford University Press, 1983).

The list should include such verbs and adjectives as these: **consist (of)**, **divide (into)**, **substitute (for)**, **ashamed (of)**, **interested (in)**, **opposed (to)**, **different (from)**.

In class the next day, students may study the sentences together, testing each other on the preposition to be used with each of the listed words.

In addition to simple definitions and illustrative sentences, the learner's dictionaries contain many other helpful features, including pictures (like the picture below, reprinted from the *Oxford Student's Dictionary of American English*[8]). When students are given the opportunities to use such a dictionary, they quickly recognize its value for increasing their comprehension of unfamiliar words.

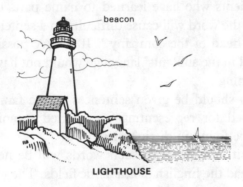

Such dictionaries can be even more helpful with words that look familiar—common verbs, for instance, like **get**, **put**, and **take** in combination with other familiar words like **in**, **on**, **up**, **over**, and **with**. Such combinations are sometimes called *phrasal verbs*.

Often a sentence that contains only familiar words will not be understood because certain *combinations* of those words have special meanings. Take this sentence, for example, "They soon **got around** to **bringing up** the question of **calling off** the meeting." Students who know all the words in that sentence may still fail to understand it. When they have been properly instructed in the use of a learner's dictionary, however, they will know that special meanings for phrasal verbs like **get around (to)**, **bring up**, and **call off** can be found in the all-English learner's dictionary.

[8]Ibid.

In the *Oxford Student's Dictionary of American English*[9] there are two pages giving definitions and examples of the verb **get**. In that dictionary, students can find special meanings for **get across**, **get ahead**, **get along**, **get around to**, and over fifty other combinations where **get** is used.

Most students will never find those pages without help, however. Students do not usually think of looking up a familiar word like **bring**, **call**, or **get**. When we introduce techniques for using dictionaries, we should teach students to look up even a word that *seems* familiar, when it appears in a sentence that is hard to understand.

Even when the familiar word is not part of a phrasal verb construction, it may cause difficulty. The word **head** is known by language students who have learned to name parts of the body; but for many the word will cause difficulty in a sentence like this: "He was the **head** of the company." It is very possible that the word for **head** in the students' language would not have this metaphorical meaning.

Students should be given sentences where familiar-looking words are used for representing unexpected meanings—which should then be found in dictionaries.

The habit of looking up such words will be needed if students are to read the English of academic fields. The word **square**, for instance, has a special meaning in mathematics; **market** has a meaning in economics that is different from its use in other contexts. Ordinary meanings are not enough to know if one wishes to read English for science and technology.

In fact, technical terms which are used only in a specialized field are sometimes less troublesome than vocabulary that looks familiar. Students recognize the *need* to find meanings for technical terms, and most dictionaries define them. On the other hand, students assume they already know the meaning of an ordinary word, so they do not try to find a specialized meaning for it.

In Advanced classes, students need to increase their vocabulary through the use of vocabulary that they have already ac-

[9]Ibid.

quired. One way of doing this has already been mentioned: the students learn new meanings for old words like **head**, **square**, and **market**. They learn that a **solution** is not only associated with a problem; it is also what results when some substance like sugar is mixed with water.

WORDS WITH MORE THAN ONE GRAMMATICAL FUNCTION

Advanced students' vocabulary can be greatly increased by awareness of the fact that certain English words have different grammatical functions in different sentences. Students at the Advanced level should learn that the word **book** is not only used as a countable noun (in familiar phrases like **a book** or **three books**); it also functions as a verb in expressions like **to book reservations at a hotel** or **to book space on an airplane**.

Particular attention should be drawn to this important feature of English, which is sometimes called *functional shift*. Often a word that is usually a noun (like **book**) may also function as a verb. The following sentence illustrates further possibilities of functional shift: "That is one of the benefits which result from space travel."

In other contexts, one may find **benefit**, **space**, and **travel** used as verbs (**to benefit from something**, **to space words on a page**, **to travel somewhere**); and the word **result**—which is a verb in the above sentence—is often used as a noun.

In Advanced classes, students and teachers should look together at such a sentence, with these questions in mind:

1. Which nouns in this sentence may also be used as verbs?
2. Which of the verbs may also be used as nouns?
3. If such a shift in function occurs, does the meaning also change? (The meaning of **to book**, for instance, is quite different from the meaning of **a book**. On the other hand, **travel** means much the same whether a noun or a verb.)

It is useful for students to know which of the words they have learned as verbs may also function as nouns without any change of form—to know that one can say, for example, "That is my **hope**" as well as "I **hope** so." To learn a new function for a word one already knows is to expand one's vocabulary in an efficient way. It is a kind of vocabulary expansion that may need to be pointed out if the students' own language *always* signals different grammatical functions by means of different endings, or by some other change in the form of the word.

Of course English, like many other languages, also has special endings and word forms that signal the grammatical function the word performs. The correspondence between forms and functions must be learned. Having learned the verbs **accept**, **allow**, and **appear**, the class learns the related nouns: **acceptance**, **allowance**, and **appearance**. (It is helpful to teach a group of **-ance** nouns like those three together, then on another day teach nouns like **announcement**, **encouragement**, and **enjoyment**, which have the **-ment** suffix in common.)

In addition to learning related verb and noun forms (like those mentioned above, or like **connect** and **connection**, **inspect** and **inspection**), Advanced classes must also learn to distinguish between noun and adjective forms, like **blood/bloody**, **glass/glassy**, **health/healthy**, and **milk/milky**. Having learned the nouns **advantage** and **courage**, they learn the adjectives **advantageous** and **courageous**.

On the other hand, if an adjective (**sad**, **dark**, or **clever**) has been learned before the noun which represents the same area of meaning, we show how a suffix (**-ness**) can be added, forming **sadness**, **darkness**, **cleverness**. The **-ly** suffix for adverbs is taught by showing that **safe** and **safely** both share the same meaning, but perform different grammatical functions. To demonstrate those functions, we give the class example sentences like the following:

That is a **safe** place to swim.
You can swim **safely** there.

For vocabulary expansion at the Advanced level, it is important to introduce the students to word families like **safe/safely/save/safety**, and **dead/die/death** (to mention just two of many such families). Yet we must also be careful to teach students which member of such a word family to use for various functions in a sentence. A student who says or writes, "Their plan did not success," has not yet learned how to choose among the members of the word family that contains **succeed**, **success**, **successful**, and **successfully**. When someone says, "He could not buy any equip for the store because of the lose of his money," there is a clear need for examples which show the respective functions of **equip** and **equipment**, **lose** and **loss**, as follows:

1. He must **equip** his new store.
   (verb)

2. He must buy some **equipment**.
   (noun)

3. Did he **lose** his money?
   (verb)

4. Who told you about the **loss** of his money?
   (noun)

When we direct attention to new words that are related to words the students have already learned, we offer the kind of help that is particularly needed at the Advanced level. As this chapter has pointed out, our two chief aims at this level are to prepare students for the kind of English used by native speakers, and to enable students to continue learning independently after their formal studies have ended. In order to accomplish those aims, the Advanced class works intensively on vocabulary expansion. Much class time is also devoted to instruction and practice in the use of a dictionary. Students should be taught
• to examine the sentence in which an unfamiliar word appears
• to find the needed page in the dictionary quickly
• to interpret symbols and abbreviations in dictionaries
• to choose intelligently among the possible meanings
In addition, we should help students discover the special aids which are offered by all-English learner's dictionaries: pictures, example sentences, simple definitions, grammatical information, and explanations of phrasal verbs (among many helpful features).

The next chapter will suggest further techniques for preparing Advanced learners to understand—and to use—the English of native speakers.

· ACTIVITIES ·

1. Answer these questions about a class that you have recently visited or taught:

1. During how much of the class period did the teacher give explanations of vocabulary words?
2. How much responsibility did the students assume for discovering word meanings?
3. What evidence did you have of the students' ability to
a. analyze a sentence before looking up an unfamiliar word in that sentence?
b. find the best meaning among several possibilities offered by the dictionary?

2. Using a dictionary that is available to your students, choose at least three symbols and/or abbreviations your class should be taught to understand.

3. Examine a copy of a dictionary (particularly the Oxford or Longman dictionary intended for ESL, if available). Find at least five features of the dictionary which could be helpful to your students.

4. Add five other verbs to the list (on page 87) of verbs usually accompanied by prepositions. Choose especially verbs which, in your students' language, would not be used with anything like prepositions.

5. Here are some English phrases in which common words are used metaphorically: the **arm** of a chair, the **leg** of the table, the

eye of the storm. Add a few more phrases that illustrate the metaphorical use of common words. (Think of phrases like the ____ of a needle, the ____ of a bottle, the long ____ of the law.)

6. Indicate whether each word in the following list is a verb, a noun, an adjective, or an adverb; and *underline* the part of the word which shows its grammatical function.

> *Example*: emphas<u>ize</u> (verb)
>
> 1. recognize   7. sadness   12. foolish
> 2. careful   8. finally   13. noisy
> 3. suggestion   9. possible   14. attractive
> 4. humorous   10. healthy   15. fortunately
> 5. dirty   11. friendship   16. lucky
> 6. punishment

7. Suppose you are teaching students to take responsibility for their own vocabulary learning. How could you use the paragraph below in a lesson intended to accomplish that purpose? (Which words in the paragraph might be unfamiliar to your Advanced students? Which words should they be able to understand from the context, without looking them up? How could you instruct them to use their dictionaries for the words which they should find there?)

> The earth is a place. It is by no means the only place. It is not even a typical place. No planet or star or galaxy can be typical, because the Cosmos is mostly empty. The only typical place is within the vast, cold, universal vacuum, the everlasting night of intergalactic space, a place so strange and desolate that, by comparison, planets and stars and galaxies seem achingly rare and lovely. If we were randomly inserted into the Cosmos, the chance that we would find ourselves on or near a planet would be less than one in a billion trillion trillion (10^{33}, a 1 followed by 33 zeroes). In everyday life such odds are called compelling. Worlds are precious.[10]

[10]Carl Sagan, *Cosmos* (New York: Random House, Inc., 1980), p. 5. Copyright © 1980 by Carl Sagan.

·CHAPTER NINE·

COMPREHENSION AND PRODUCTION IN ADVANCED CLASSES

Several times in these chapters the point has been made that *a word is most likely to be learned when the learner feels a personal need to know it*. Sometimes a learner feels the need to learn certain words because those words hold essential keys to *understanding* something interesting or important. At other times the feeling of need is induced by the desire to *express* something, to produce phrases and sentences that accomplish the learner's own purposes.

The following example will show how the desire for comprehension can lead to vocabulary learning. Suppose someone reads a horoscope that states, "People who were born on July 3rd are generous and extravagant. They are usually very popular with members of the opposite sex; it is easy to love them. Although artistic and creative, they have certain faults. They are sometimes obstinate and often gullible." If the reader of the horoscope was born on July 3rd, any unfamiliar words it contains (such as **extravagant**, **obstinate**, and **gullible**) will almost surely be looked up and learned.

At the Advanced level of instruction, the sense of need for a word is often induced by reading. Vocabulary is learned through reading something that students really want to understand, or something they know they must understand for some reason important to them. When most of the material is understood—when the proportion of unknown words is not discouragingly large—students generally learn those unfamiliar words.

Chapter 8 stressed the importance of showing students how

to deal intelligently with the unfamiliar words found in their reading. In that chapter we emphasized the need to show students how their acquaintance with a word (**enjoy**, for example) can lead to the learning of new words (like **enjoyment, enjoyable**, and **enjoyably**) where endings such as **-ment, -able** and **-ly** signal different grammatical functions for members of a word family. Such endings, which are sometimes called *derivational suffixes*, deserve attention, especially in Advanced classes, for two reasons. One is that students' comprehension of English can be greatly strengthened by recognizing familiar elements within words they have not seen before. The other is that their production of English sentences often depends on knowing correspondences between word forms and grammatical functions (or parts of speech). Without that knowledge, the learner tends to use the wrong member of a word family—to say, for example, "That was a very enjoy party."

As we have seen, new words which have been formed by adding suffixes to familiar vocabulary are introduced in simple sentences like the following:

1. He is **kind** and **good**.
      (adj.)   (adj.)
We appreciate his **kindness** and **goodness**.
                  (noun)   (noun)

2.   Schools **educate** children. They provide **education**.
              (verb)   (noun)

3. There is **dirt** on the floor. The floor is **dirty**.
          (noun)   (adj.)

4. He is **careful**. He works **carefully**.
          (adj.)   (adverb)

It is wise to begin with just a few suffixes which are very commonly used and to combine them with words that the students already know. Once the students have formed the habit of looking for familiar elements within longer unfamiliar words, they will go on to discover other suffixes for themselves.

In addition to teaching suffixes, we show our Advanced students how their vocabulary can be expanded through acquaintance with certain commonly used prefixes. When the words

happy, **important**, and **pleasant** have been learned, the class can quickly acquire **unhappy**, **unimportant**, and **unpleasant**. Having learned that the prefix **un-** means *not*, the students can learn that **in-**, **il-**, **im-**, **ir-** also represent *not* in words like **incomplete**, **illegal**, **imperfect**, and **irregular**.

As with suffixes, we do not attempt to teach all existing prefixes. We show how a few of the more common ones can be added to known words, and we put the examples into sentences like these:

1. A **trans**continental train is a train that goes **across** a continent.
2. **Sub**standard quality is quality that is **below** standard.
3. To **re**heat something is to heat it **again**.
4. A **pre**historic animal is an animal that lived **before** history began.
5. A machine that **mal**functions is a machine that functions **poorly**.

Small-group Activities Related to Prefixes, Suffixes, and Word Families

Like Intermediate students, Advanced students benefit from opportunities to work in small groups on tasks involving cooperative effort. For each task there should be a leader, who holds an answer card that has been prepared by the teacher. Here are some small-group activities that provide practice with prefixes, suffixes, and word families.

TASK 1:

One of the listed words is needed for completing each sentence. The <u>underlined</u> <u>prefix</u> will tell you which word is needed.

across   again   poorly   before   below

1. A <u>sub</u>way does not go above a city; it goes <u>below</u>.
2. <u>Mal</u>adjusted people are people who adjust ____.
3. A <u>trans</u>atlantic flight goes ____ the Atlantic.
4. A <u>pre</u>fix is a word-part that comes ____.
5. When we <u>re</u>write something, we write it ____.

6. A <u>sub</u>normal temperature is not above normal, it is ____.

7. To <u>pre</u>arrange something is to arrange it in advance, or ____.

8. To <u>re</u>copy a composition is to copy it ____.

TASK 2:

Here are noun forms that correspond to the <u>underlined</u> adjectives in the following sentences. Fill each blank with the appropriate noun. Then copy each completed sentence.

Nouns:

death	depth	height
pride	strength	warmth
width	youth	

1. After you find out how <u>wide</u> the room is, write its <u>width</u> here.

2. I know the river is <u>deep</u>, but I don't know its exact ____.

3. He is <u>proud</u>, and there are good reasons for his ____.

4. <u>Young</u> people seldom appreciate their ____.

5. Is this <u>wide</u> enough, or should I increase the ____?

6. She told us he was <u>dead</u>, but she didn't tell us the cause of his ____.

7. Sometimes a <u>strong</u> man is not aware of his own ____.

8. I don't know how <u>high</u> that ceiling is, but I'm going to measure its ____.

9. The kitchen was <u>warm</u>, and we all appreciated the ____.

10. My <u>young</u> cousin knows a lot, in spite of his ____.

TASK 3:

The words in parentheses before each of the following sentences all belong to the same word family, but only one of those words belongs in the blank. Decide what *kind* of word belongs there:

verb, noun, adjective, or adverb. Then take the right word from the parentheses and copy the completed sentence.

1. (**depend, dependable, dependably**)
Their new helper is very ＿＿.
2. (**satisfaction, satisfactory, satisfactorily**)
He has completed the work ＿＿.
3. (**beauty, beautiful, beautifully**)
Everyone admires goodness and ＿＿.
4. (**collect, collection, collective**)
When do they ＿＿ the mail?
5. (**artist, artistic, artistically**)
Her niece is very ＿＿.
6. (**destroy, destruction, destructive**)
The fire produced terrible ＿＿ everywhere.
7. (**gratitude, grateful, gratefully**)
How can we express our ＿＿?
8. (**science, scientific, scientifically**)
Your reasons are not very ＿＿.
9. (**explain, explanation, explanatory**)
What is his ＿＿?
10. (**repeat, repetition, repetitive**
Sometimes ＿＿ helps us.

In stressing activities that relate new words (and word forms) to words already learned, we draw attention to the need to expand Advanced students' vocabulary—particularly by showing them how they will be able to discover word meanings for themselves when there is no longer a teacher to help them. Activities which are designed to develop independence among students do take time. Some readers may think, "It takes time to train students to use dictionaries. And how can we find time for group-study or discussions by members of the class? After all, there are *so many words* to be taught in the Advanced class. How could there be time for anything more?"

The fact is, however, that we cannot possibly *teach* all the words a student must know. Even in classes where most of the time is used for explanations of vocabulary, the teacher can never give students a command of all the words they will need. Each student must be responsible for much of his own learning. Consequently, the teacher's chief task is to show students how to use the tools available to them. When students have been taught how to deal intelligently with words they need, they can continue to learn vocabulary for the rest of their lives.

LEARNING ADVANCED VOCABULARY FOR USE

Much vocabulary in the Advanced class is learned for *comprehension* of what is being read. However, there are also words to be learned for the students' own *use* (or *production*) in speaking and writing.

Here are some class activities which require the use of English words for communication:

Paraphrases and Summaries
Students are asked to express—in simpler and briefer form—the main ideas of an article or an essay, orally or in writing. (To do so, students must learn words from the original article and also obtain other words for expressing the ideas in sentences of their own.)

Group Compositions
The class is organized into small groups. All groups are assigned the same topic (some topic that makes use of the students' own experience, like "Bicycle Safety," or "How to Study for an Examination"). Working together, the members of each group compose a paragraph or two on the assigned topic. One member writes the composition as the others dictate it. Two or three of the compositions are then copied on the blackboard. They are chosen by the teacher, who has walked around observing the work and given help as requested.

Letters to Speakers of English
The very best way to learn vocabulary is to have a friend with whom it is necessary and interesting to use English. In many

places where English is studied, there is no easy way to arrange for friendships between language students and speakers of English. However, it is often possible to arrange for an exchange of letters. Fortunately, there are responsible organizations which provide names and addresses of young persons interested in becoming pen pals. One such organization is World Pen Pals (1690 Como Avenue, c/o International Institute, St. Paul, Minnesota 55108). Individuals who use this service pay approximately $1.00; special rates are available for groups.

In some ESL classes, the students and the teacher together compose a letter to be sent to a class in an English-speaking country. Sometimes several of the students have their own pen pals, whose letters are shared with members of the ESL class.

When such an exchange of letters is possible, it has many uses. ESL students can obtain from their English-speaking correspondents much information not found in books. The social meanings of vocabulary words can be learned by asking questions about the correspondents' everyday lives. (Appendix D lists questions that can be included for this purpose in letters to pen pals.)

Most of all, the exchange of letters has the value of encouraging ESL students to express their own thoughts and ideas by means of English. In attempting to do this, they will learn many useful English words.

A Wall Newspaper

Members of the class contribute articles and other items to a "newspaper" which is taped to the classroom wall. The newspaper should have a name (such as *The Classroom Times*) and an editor and several reporters. It should be "published" at frequent and regular intervals. In addition to news, various sections of the paper might include sports items, pictures, cartoons, social notes, advertisements, editorials, recipes, advice on teenage problems, letters to the editor, and other features commonly found in newspapers intended for speakers of English.

Situational and Functional Dialogs

Whether or not there are opportunities for using English with native speakers of the language, the class can be engaged in *imagined* or *simulated* experiences that require the use of English. Students should be asked to write and then to present to their classmates various kinds of dialogs.

Some should be related to situations: at the post office, in a restaurant, at the airport, in a bookstore, in a hotel, and so on. (In most classes, there are a few students who are particularly imaginative. Those students may find it interesting to act the part of tourists who speak English. Working with one or two classmates, they prepare dialogs that might take place in various situations; then the dialogs should be read aloud to the class.)

At other times, students may be asked to write dialogs in which the speakers use English for performing such functions as the following:

• requesting a favor
• apologizing for something
• making an appointment with a doctor, dentist, or some other professional person
• inviting someone to do something
• complaining politely about something

Teachers who are native speakers of English can show students how to express ideas more idiomatically. But the teacher who is not a native speaker should also encourage students to write situational and functional dialogs.

Whether or not English is the teacher's native language, the students should be told that their dialogs will not be "corrected" in detail. The chief aims of the activity are

1. to encourage students to discover how much they can say in English, and
2. to show students what remains to be learned.

When students have confidence in their ability to use English, they find ways to continue learning beyond the Advanced course.

·ACTIVITIES·

1. Write sentences (similar to those on page 95) which could help your students relate the new words: **cruelty**, **generosity**, **poverty**, and **necessity**, to the adjective forms they already know: **cruel**, **generous**, **poor**, and **necessary**.

2. Write an exercise like Task 2 on page 97. Use the same instructions, but list the following nouns in place of those listed in Task 2: **breadth**, **comfort**, **curiosity**, **difference**, **difficulty**, **permanence**, **poison**, **sincerity**. For each of those nouns, write a sentence like the ones in Task 2, where the underlined adjective gives a clue to the choice of the noun for filling the blank.

3. Suppose a student who has just joined your class seems to be confused about the uses of the words **arrive**, **arrival**; **choose**, **choice**; and **advise**, **advice**. Write illustrative sentences that could help that student understand how each of those words should be used.

4. We can encourage students to look for familiar words within unfamiliar longer ones by asking them to complete such sentences as these:

    1. A person who is **ungrateful** is not <u>(grateful)</u>.

    2. An **inconvenient** time is a time that is not <u>(convenient)</u>.

    3. An **irregular** heartbeat is one that is not <u>(regular)</u>.

Add seven more sentences like these to show students how the prefix contributes to the meanings of the words **unafraid**, **unattractive**, **incomplete**, **indefinite**, **impossible**, **illiterate**, and **irresponsible**.

5. Mention three topics that could be used for *group compositions*. (Like the topics suggested on page 99, your topics should make use of the students' own experience.)

6. Write a short letter which your students could use as a model for letters to pen pals. In the letter, include five questions from Appendix D, "Questions for Conversations and Correspondence with Native Speakers."

7. If your students are interested in horoscopes, plan a lesson in which horoscopes (in English) are read as a means of making a few unfamiliar words seem interesting and important to the individual reader.

·CHAPTER TEN·
BEFORE AND AFTER TEACHING

Chapters 2 through 9 have suggested techniques for teaching vocabulary at various levels of instruction. These chapters have offered answers to the basic question of how we teach vocabulary. This final chapter will consider answers to two additional questions that might be raised at any time during the instructional program. The first question is, Which words do students most need to learn? (This is something to think about before teaching any lesson.) The other question comes after we have taught. We then ask, How can we know that the needed vocabulary has been mastered?

HOW TO CHOOSE THE WORDS MOST IMPORTANT TO KNOW

No one knows exactly how many English words must be learned for a real command of the language. Approximately 30,000 is the number which is often mentioned. That is the approximate number of words to be understood by anyone who reads newspapers, magazines, and books of general interest to speakers of English.

Notice the phrase "of general interest." The figure 30,000 does not include terms which are found only in technical books and journals. If such words were included, the figure would be very much larger.

To the ESL teacher, even the number 30,000 seems discouraging. Imagine helping a student learn so many words! It sounds impossible.

Of course, students do not have to learn to *use* all these words in their own speaking and writing. For many of the 30,000 words, understanding is enough. Students need only understand them when they meet them in the sentences they read or hear. Even in our own native language, we recognize and understand many more words than we say or write. In time, some words which we have learned for comprehension (or recognition) become part of our active (or productive) vocabulary. But there are many that never do.

This is comforting to keep in mind when we talk about teaching 30,000 English words. Only a much smaller number (perhaps no more than 3,000) will be necessary "productive" items. Those are the ones to be learned thoroughly enough to be used in the students' own writing and speech.

In most English programs, the work of selecting the important words has already been done by the writer of the textbook. Some books, however, are not very helpful in their choice of vocabulary. This is especially true of some books published long ago. It may also be true of some by writers who are not native speakers of the language being taught.

At times, too, there is no book at all for the class. At such times, teachers have to depend on their own judgment for answers to the question: Which words must the class be especially sure to learn?

Even where there is a good textbook, we cannot give equal attention to all the words in the lessons. How do we choose the most important ones? One measure of importance is *frequency of use*. If students are going to meet a word frequently in their reading of English, that word is important to learn. In the following sentence, for instance, several of the words must be learned by students because of the frequency with which they appear in English: "You and I are considering the significance of frequency in weighing the importance of a lexical item." In this sentence, the most frequent words are the pronouns **you** and **I**, the conjunction **and**, the auxiliary **are**, the articles **the** and **a**, and the prepositions **in** and **of**. (The article **the** and the preposition **of** occur more than once in this sentence, as they do in millions of English sentences.)

Pronouns, prepositions, auxiliaries, articles, and conjunctions are closely related to the grammar of English, so they are usually taught during the part of the class period that focuses on grammar. Techniques for teaching grammar are suggested in a different volume of this series.

Although the most frequently used words are pronouns, prepositions, articles, auxiliaries, and conjunctions, there are also many nouns, verbs, adjectives, and adverbs which are used so frequently that students are very likely to meet them in their reading of English. For instance, it is quite obvious that the noun **man** is used more often than **gentleman** or **fellow**, and the verb **get** is more common than **obtain** or **acquire**. There would be value, some teachers think, in having a list that would contain all the words most important to learn, from the standpoint of frequency. Let us consider some difficulties that arise from the listing of words frequently used.

The Limitations of Word Lists

Teachers (and those who write textbooks or syllabuses) often wish they could find a dependable list showing all the words that are most frequently used. The most famous list is *The Teacher's Word Book of 30,000 Words* by Edward L. Thorndike and Irving Lorge. But that book was published in 1944. At that time, **king** and **lady** were among the 500 words most frequently found in many different kinds of books and magazines. Today those words are less commonly used. On the other hand, **drug** and **sex** were rare words in 1944, and **nuclear** did not appear among the 30,000 at all. If we were to use the Thorndike-Lorge list as the chief guide to our selection of most important words, we would therefore spend too much time on words less frequently used today, and we would fail to teach words that have become very frequent since that list was compiled.

Even lists which were prepared much more recently than the Thorndike list cannot be depended on for guidance in selecting words to teach. To see why that is true, we will take as an example the results of a study made in the United States during the 1970s. The aim was to find out which English words were known by

American children in different school grades. After years of work with thousands of children, the results of the study were published by Edgar Dale and Joseph O'Rourke in a book, *The Living Word Vocabulary: The Words We Know*.[11] The book tells what happened when vocabulary tests were given to American students in various grades.

At first glance, it might seem that a list of words known by most American school children would be valuable to teachers of ESL. Particularly, one might think there would be value in a list of words known by English-speaking fourth-graders (pupils approximately ten years old). One reason for assuming such a list would be useful is that children in many countries begin to study ESL at the age of ten or eleven. Furthermore, the fourth grade is the grade in which American children generally start to read textbooks in content areas like history, geography, and science. The Dale-O'Rourke report shows which words those children bring to their reading of books that give them information about the world. Since ESL students also hope to learn about the world through reading English, the report on fourth-graders' known vocabulary should have special significance. On examining the list of words found in *The Living Word Vocabulary*, however, one sees how wrong it would be to use such a list as the basis for planning vocabulary lessons in ESL. Students of a foreign language can never hope to acquire all the words that native speakers know, even native speakers in the fourth grade. Some English words known by pupils at a certain school grade may *never* be learned by ESL students. Indeed, they may never even be needed. Examples include **achoo** (which represents the sound of a sneeze) and **tummy** (a child's word for **stomach**).

As we have seen, then, lists of words are not reliable guides to the selection of words to be taught. Even when the list is the result of careful work by scholars like Thorndike and Lorge or Dale and O'Rourke, there are reasons why it should not control our decisions about vocabulary to be introduced in our lessons.

[11]Edgar Dale and Joseph O'Rourke, *The Living Word Vocabulary: The Words We Know* (Elgin, Illinois: Dome Press, 1976).

Perhaps the list was compiled too long ago to give an accurate picture of vocabulary that is important today. Perhaps it was prepared for a purpose which is different from our purposes. These are among the many reasons why we should not use any existing list as a basis for teaching vocabulary, although certain lists are worth looking at from time to time. A carefully compiled list can be useful for *reference*, and it can serve as *one of several* factors to take into account in deciding which words should be given more emphasis than other words. Consequently, we have listed "Three Hundred Useful Adjectives" in Appendix B (pages 119-20) and "Twelve Hundred Useful Nouns and Verbs" in Appendix C (pages 121-27). Each of the words has been taken from one or more internationally known lists, which are named on page 119. As we have emphasized in this chapter, however, *no* list should be used for deciding which words to teach our students. A better guide is a set of questions like the following:

 1. Which words must the students know in order to talk about people, things, and events in the place where they study and live? (When such words are learned, the new language can immediately be put to use.)

 2. Which words must the students know in order to respond to routine directions and commands? (The vocabulary for "Open your books" and "Write these sentences" and other routine instructions should be learned early, so that such frequently repeated directions can always be given in English.)

 3. Which words are required for certain classroom experiences (describing, comparing, and classifying various animals, for example, or having imaginary conversations with speakers of English, or writing letters to pen pals)?

 4. Which words are needed in connection with the students' particular academic interests? (Those who will specialize in science need vocabulary that is different from those who plan business careers.)

Such questions help us decide which words need special attention among the thousands that speakers of English know.

HOW TO FIND OUT WHICH WORDS THE STUDENTS KNOW

When we start the school year with a new group of Intermediate or Advanced students, it is helpful to know which members of the class have already learned more vocabulary than their classmates. They can serve as helpers and leaders, and the students who most need to learn vocabulary can be given special kinds of work.

At the end of the school year, a test can help to show how much has been achieved by individuals in the class. When an achievement test is given at various times during the school term, it can tell the teacher something about students' progress in learning the needed words. Moreover—as we all certainly know—those who are responsible for a language program often require some evidence of students' learning. Scores on tests are considered important when the value of a program is being weighed.

As many teachers have discovered, however, certain kinds of tests are better than others. There are some tests that give us little helpful information about a student's actual knowledge of vocabulary.

In many tests, the student is asked to look at a word and to choose some word with the same meaning from among three or four listed possibilities. An item on such a test looks like this:

brief: fair   loud   short   warm

The expected answer, of course, is **short**. Students who make the right choice may really know the meanings of **brief**, **fair**, **loud**, **short**, and **warm**. But it is also possible that some of those students have merely made a lucky guess. On the other hand, some students who fail to choose **short** (as a synonym for **brief**) might actually understand sentences in which **brief** and **short** are used. The ability to do that is the important thing. It is much less important to be able to choose a synonym from a given list.

When the test involves choosing antonyms (words with *opposite* meanings) the test scores should be trusted even less. Suppose a student is asked to find an antonym for **cruel** in the following list: **fine**, **merry**, **stubborn**, **kind**. It is possible that a student with quite a good understanding of **cruel** may fail to choose the expected answer because of some such reasoning as this: "I know the words **fine**, **merry**, and **kind**. They are very different from **cruel**. A cruel person could never be called **fine** or **kind**, and I'm sure no cruel person could be **merry**. I've never seen the word **stubborn** before. Maybe it's the right answer—a word even more opposite than the other three. I'd better choose **stubborn**."

Of course that student's wrong choice does not tell us he has failed to learn the meaning of **cruel**, even though the test was intended to give us that sort of information.

Why Certain Tests Do Not Show What Students Know

When we ask students to give synonyms or antonyms, we ask them to demonstrate skills that are needed for *teaching* a language or for writing dictionaries. Such skills are not needed for speaking, reading, or writing in the practical situations where language is used.

The same point applies to another kind of exercise often used for finding out whether a student knows a certain word. Students are sometimes asked to use a certain word in a sentence for the purpose of showing its meaning or use. This is a skill needed by *teachers*. A language teacher should always be able and ready to put a word into an example sentence. But people who do not teach language have little need for that skill. Students with quite satisfactory vocabularies may not be able to compose good example sentences upon request. A student who actually knows the word **satisfactory**, for instance, may be unable to use **satisfactory** in a sentence when requested to do so.

Furthermore, even when such a sentence has been composed by the student, it is hard to decide what the sentence shows about his understanding of the word. Suppose his sentence is this: "Your plan is satisfactory," or this: "Everyone likes satisfactory houses." Would either sentence show that the student knows the difference between **satisfactory** and **interesting** or **convenient**? Does either sentence tell us he can understand **satisfactory** when he meets it in his reading?

We learn little about students' command of vocabulary by

asking them to use new words in sentences. Even native speakers' minds become blank when they are asked to make up sentences without relation to reality.

The problem, then, is to find a really dependable way of testing vocabulary. Probably *no* test which can be given in a classroom will provide a true picture of what the student knows. The form of a test is too different from the situations where communication occurs in life. Nevertheless, we often *must* use vocabulary tests, and some kinds are better than others.

Some Better Types of Tests
In one of the better kinds, the student is given two or three paragraphs in which several words are <u>underlined</u>. The purpose is to discover which of the underlined words the student understands. For example, one such paragraph may look like this:

> For some reason Richard West has been having great <u>difficulty</u> in getting to sleep lately. Last night he
> 1
> thought it might help if he went to bed even earlier than usual, so at 9:30 he lay down, <u>closed</u> his eyes hopefully,
> 2
> and began counting sheep. Thinking of all those <u>energetic</u> little animals jumping over fences made him
> 3
> feel energetic himself, so he stopped, went downstairs, and found the most <u>boring</u> book he had. It was a book
> 4
> called *Home <u>Rug-Making</u>*.[12]
> 5

After reading the paragraph, the student is asked to find words whose meanings correspond to the meanings of the underlined words, choosing from the following list (which in some programs may be in the students' language): **carpet, desire, dress,**

---

[12]O'Neill, *English in Situations*, p. 176.

lively, necessary, rubbed, shut, trouble, uninteresting. (Notice that some extra words are included here, to reduce the chance of merely *guessing* right.)

If a student decides that **difficulty** (the first underlined word in the paragraph) has a meaning close to **trouble**, we know something important about his practical command of vocabulary. We know that he would probably understand a sentence in his reading where **difficulty** appeared. Such a test also gives useful information about a student who chooses **dress** (instead of **carpet**) for the underlined word **rug** in the last sentence.

In a somewhat different type of vocabulary test, the student uses a paragraph from which some words have been omitted. A blank space indicates where each omitted word belongs. The student must find the omitted word in an alphabetized list which is given below the paragraph.

Here is how the paragraph about Richard West could be used in a *cloze* test (where students find words that are needed for completing sentences):

For some reason Richard West has been having

great _____ in getting to sleep lately. Last night he
        1

thought it might help if he went to bed even earlier than

usual, so at 9:30 he _____ down, closed his eyes hope-
                    2

fully, and began counting sheep. Thinking of all those

energetic little _____ jumping over fences made him feel
                3

energetic himself, so he _____, went downstairs, and
                         4

found the most boring book he had. It was a book _____
                                                 5

Home Rug-Making.

The numbered blanks are to be filled by choosing from the following alphabetized list: **animals, called, children, difficulty, fell, fun, lay, slept, stopped**. (Notice that only one of the listed words could properly be used in each blank, and some words are not needed for any blank.)

A fairly true picture of students' vocabulary can generally be obtained from scores on such tests. In addition, certain uses of dictation can also help us find out which words the students actually know. Here is one such use of dictation for vocabulary testing:

On a blank sheet of paper, the student writes his name and these numbers:

1.   6.
2.   7.
3.   8.
4.   9.
5.   10.

The students are told they will be asked to write a word beside each number; the teacher will tell them which words to write. The words will all be related to a picture (or a series of pictures) which the teacher will show them. (In this way, a *context* is provided— just as the paragraphs provided context for vocabulary selection in the tests which have just been described.)

In English, then—while displaying the large picture—the teacher says: "Let's look at this picture of a circus. We can see the lions and tigers and the other circus animals and the clowns and the acrobats. They're all in a tent where there are many people. Now I'm going to say some words that are related to this picture. You will write each word after I say it. The first word is **circus**; write **circus** beside number one . . . ; number two, **tent**, that's where the animals and the people are. The next word, number three, is **clown**," and so on, until ten words have been dictated and written.

Although dictation usually serves as a test of spelling, it can also measure vocabulary knowledge. In most cases, words cannot be written from dictation unless the writer has some familiarity with them. (If this seems doubtful, try asking some friend who speaks a different language to dictate words from his language to you.)

Tests which show vocabulary *in context* (in sentences and paragraphs—or in relation to pictures) are better than other kinds. However, even the best available measures of language learning are far from perfect. Scores on classroom tests will always show only part of what the student knows. We can get a better picture of students' progress by observing them at work in class each day. (Chapters 2 through 9 have described classroom activities that call for the *use* of vocabulary. Such activities can serve as measures of vocabulary mastery—better measures than the typical paper-and-pencil test.)

The best measure of language learning may not be found in the language class at all. The real test comes in situations outside that class, when words which are needed are remembered and used. In moments of practical need, the learner finds words that may have seemed lost.

Fortunately, this happens more often than teachers expect. It happens most when the teacher has encouraged *communication* in class through experiences requiring English words.

·ACTIVITIES·

1. Teachers often have to decide which words in a reading selection should be learned for production (for the students' own speech and writing) and which ones need only be understood. Read the following paragraph, and then answer the questions below the paragraph.

TELEVISION PROGRAMS

Often eight or more people are needed to create a television program. Each carefully prepares for his part in the show, and he knows his job well. The day for the filming finally arrives. The set is finished at last. It is cleared of all except the actors, the card boys, and those who operate the cameras and sound booms. All of the actors arrive early in the morning to practice the program once more.[13]

1. In your opinion, which of the underlined words in that paragraph will students probably *not* need to use in their own speech and writing? List those words, and write "For Comprehension" above the list.

[13]*Book 6*, Progressive Reading Series (Washington, D.C.: United States Information Agency, 1975), p. 37. Adapted from *TV Window on the World*, by Charles I. Coombs. Copyright © 1965 by Charles I. Coombs. Reprinted from the Ladder edition of the same title.

2. Here are some pairs of words from the paragraph. In your opinion, which of the paired words would be *more* important for your students to learn? That is, which word would be more useful to them for their own speaking and writing?

    a. **cameras** or **sound booms**?
    b. **finished** or **cleared**?
    c. **card boys** or **actors**?
    d. **arrive** or **operate**?

2. Examine a textbook which is used in your English program, and try to guess why the author of the text selected the vocabulary that appears in the lessons. (The questions listed on page 108 of this chapter will suggest some reasons. For instance, you should be able to find several words in the textbook which were included because of students' need to talk about people and things in the place where they study and live.)

3. Through experience in teaching ESL, we learn which words are probably known by students at different levels of instruction. (Some new teachers also have this useful skill.) When we can communicate with students by using English words that they already know, we do not have to use their mother tongue for explanations.

The following pairs of words are not exact synonyms, but their meanings are similar. In your opinion, which word of the pair would more probably be known by students in their second year of ESL study?

    a. **sleep** or **nap**?   e. **shrub** or **tree**?
    b. **slim** or **thin**?   f. **prosperous** or **rich**?
    c. **soft** or **smooth**?   g. **interesting** or **fascinating**?
    d. **grasp** or **take**?   h. **hotel** or **inn**?

4. Look at a vocabulary test which is sometimes given to students of ESL in your school. What does the test ask the students to do? Which of the tasks mentioned in this chapter are found on that test? In how many parts of the test are students asked to make judgments about a word without seeing it in sentence context?

Which of the skills that are being tested are really skills for *teachers* (not for all who use English as a means of communication)?

5. Prepare a vocabulary test similar to the type illustrated on page 111, where words are underlined in a paragraph and students choose from among listed synonyms for the underlined words.

6. Using the same paragraph that you chose for Activity 5, show how you might use it for a cloze test (where students find words for completing the sentences, as illustrated on page 112). Which words would you omit from the paragraph when it is used for this type of test?

7. Explain how you could use *dictation* (in relation to a large picture) for testing vocabulary, as illustrated on page 113.

8. In your own experience as a teacher and learner of languages, what are the best ways of discovering which words have really been learned?

TEN PICTURABLE ACTIONS

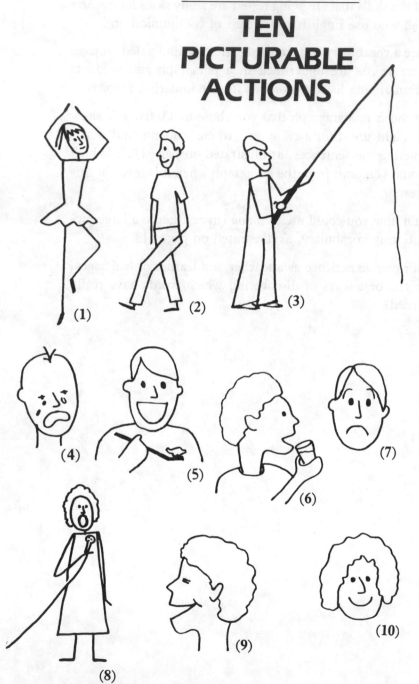

(4) crying

(1) dancing

(6) drinking

(5) eating

(3) fishing

(7) frowning

(9) laughing

(10) smiling

(8) singing

(2) walking

· APPENDIX B ·

THREE HUNDRED USEFUL ADJECTIVES*

absent	charming	different	final
afraid	cheap	difficult	fine
alive	cheerful	direct	flat
alone	chemical	dirty	foolish
angry	chief	double	foreign
ashamed	clean	dry	formal
asleep	clear	dull	fortunate
attractive	clever		free
available	cloudy	eager	fresh
average	cold	early	full
aware	comfortable	easy	funny
awful	common	electric	future
	complete	elementary	
bad	complex	empty	general
basic	constant	entire	generous
beautiful	convenient	equal	gentle
big	cool	essential	glad
black	correct	exact	good
blank	crazy	excellent	gradual
blind	cruel	extra	grand
blue	curious		grateful
brief		fair	gray
bright	dangerous	false	great
broad	dark	familiar	green
brown	dead	famous	
busy	deaf	far	handsome
	dear	fast	happy
calm	deep	fat	hard
careful	definite	favorite	healthy
careless	delicious	female	heavy

*These adjectives appear on one or more of the following lists: *The 5,000 Words of the Ladder Series* (U.S. Information Agency, n.d.), Michael West's *A General Service List of English Words* (Longman, 1953, reprinted 1977). *2,000 Words Used in Explanations and Examples in the Longman Dictionary of Contemporary English* (Longman, 1978) and *Words Used in the Voice of America's Special English Broadcasts* (U.S. Information Agency, 1964).

high	married	queer	sudden
honest	marvelous	quick	sure
hot	maximum	quiet	
huge	mere		terrible
human	merry	rare	thick
hungry		raw	thin
	narrow	ready	thirsty
ideal	natural	recent	thorough
ill	neat	red	tight
imaginary	necessary	regular	tiny
important	negative	responsible	tired
impossible	neutral	rich	total
independent	new	right	tough
individual	nice	ripe	tragic
innocent	noisy	rough	tropical
insane		round	true
instant	obvious	rural	typical
intelligent	odd		
interested	official	sad	ugly
interesting	old	safe	universal
international	open	scientific	unusual
irregular	opposite	secret	urban
	original	separate	urgent
jealous	outstanding	serious	usual
juicy		sharp	
junior	pale	short	vacant
just	particular	sick	valuable
	past	silent	various
large	perfect	similar	vast
late	permanent	simple	violent
lazy	personal	sincere	vital
left	plain	single	
legal	pleasant	sleepy	warm
light	poisonous	slow	weak
little	polite	small	welcome
local	poor	smooth	wet
lonely	popular	social	white
long	potential	soft	whole
loose	practical	sore	wicked
loud	present	sorry	wide
lovely	pretty	sour	wild
low	principal	special	willing
luck	private	steady	wonderful
	probable	straight	wrong
mad	professional	strange	
main	proud	strong	yellow
major	public	stupid	young
male	pure	successful	

TWELVE HUNDRED USEFUL NOUNS AND VERBS*

NOTES:

Useful nouns which are not listed here include names of days, months, states, countries, continents, and numbers.

Many of the listed words can serve as both nouns and verbs.

The number 1200 is approximate; the exact number cannot be determined without sentence context to show the number of meanings for a word like **bank**, **drop**, **figure**, **iron**, **line**, or **mind** (among many others).

accept	apple	bake	bit
accident	apply	balance	bite
accompany	appoint	ball	blame
account	area	band	blank
act	argue	bank	blanket
action	arm	bar	bless
add	army	base	block
admire	arrange	basis	blood
admit	arrive	basket	blow
advance	art	bath	board
advantage	article	battle	boat
adventure	artist	bag	body
advice	ask	beach	boil
advise	association	bear	bone
afford	assume	beat	book
afternoon	attack	beauty	bottle
age	attempt	become	bottom
agree	attend	bed	box
aid	attention	beg	boy
aim	attitude	begin	brain
air	aunt	belief	branch
allow	author	believe	bread
amount	automobile	bell	break
anger	autumn	belong	breakfast
animal	avenue	belt	breath
announce	avoid	bend	breathe
answer		benefit	bridge
apartment	baby	bill	bring
appeal	back	bird	brook
appear	bag	birth	brother

*Each of these words appears on one or more of the lists named in Appendix B.

brush	circle	cotton	department
build	circumstance	council	depend
building	citizen	count	describe
burn	city	country	desert
burst	claim	couple	deserve
bury	class	courage	desire
bush	climate	course	desk
business	climb	cousin	destroy
butter	clock	cover	detail
button	close	cow	develop
buy	cloth	cream	die
	clothes	create	difference
cake	clothing	credit	difficulty
call	cloud	crime	dig
camp	coast	crop	dignity
can	coat	cross	dinner
candy	coffee	crowd	direction
capital	collect	crush	director
car	color	cry	disappear
card	column	cup	discover
care	comb	cure	discuss
carry	combine	curl	disease
case	come	curse	dish
cash	comfort	curtain	display
cat	command	curve	distance
catch	committee	custom	district
cattle	company	cut	divide
cause	compare		do
cent	concern	dance	doctor
center	condition	danger	dog
century	conduct	dare	doll
chain	confidence	date	dollar
chair	connect	daughter	door
chance	consider	day	dot
change	consist	debt	doubt
chapter	constitution	death	dozen
character	contain	decide	draw
charge	continent	decision	dream
cheek	continue	declare	dress
cheese	control	defeat	drink
chest	conversation	defend	drive
chicken	cook	degree	drop
child	copy	delay	drug
children	corn	delight	drum
choice	corner	deliver	dust
choose	correct	demand	duty
church	cost	deny	

ear	experiment	floor	go
earn	explain	flour	god
earth	explanation	flow	gold
east	express	flower	got
eat	expression	fluid	govern
edge	extend	fly	government
editor	eye	fold	grade
educate		folks	grain
education	face	follow	grandfather
effect	fact	food	grandmother
effort	factory	fool	grape
egg	fail	foot	grasp
elbow	fall	force	grief
elect	family	forehead	ground
election	farm	forest	grow
electricity	fashion	forget	guard
element	fate	forgive	guess
elephant	father	form	guest
emotion	fault	fortune	guide
encourage	favor	foundation	gulf
end	fear	fountain	gun
enemy	feather	frame	
energy	feature	freeze	habit
engine	feed	friend	had
engineer	feel	frighten	hair
enjoy	fellow	front	half
enter	female	fruit	hall
entrance	fence	fun	hand
environment	fever	funeral	handkerchief
equal	field	fur	handle
error	fight	furniture	hang
escape	figure	future	happen
establish	fill		happiness
evening	film	gain	harbor
event	find	game	harm
examine	finger	garden	harvest
example	finish	gas	has
exception	fire	gate	hat
exchange	fish	gather	hate
excite	fit	gentleman	have
exclaim	fix	get	head
excuse	flag	giant	health
exercise	flame	gift	hear
exist	flesh	girl	heart
expect	flight	glance	heat
expense	float	glass	heaven
experience	flood	glove	heel

height	insist	lady	lose
hell	instance	lake	loss
help	institution	lamb	lot
hesitate	instruction	lamp	love
hide	instrument	land	luck
hill	intend	language	lunch
hire	intention	last	
history	interest	laugh	machine
hit	interrupt	laughter	magazine
hold	introduce	law	magic
hole	invent	lawyer	mail
holiday	invention	lay	make
home	invitation	lead	male
honey	invite	learn	man
honor	iron	leather	manage
hook	island	leave	manner
hope		left	manufacture
horn	jacket	leg	map
horse	jar	lend	march
hospital	jeans	length	mark
hotel	jewel	lesson	market
hour	job	let	marriage
house	join	letter	marry
humor	joke	level	mass
hunger	journey	liberty	master
hunt	joy	lie	match
hurry	judge	life	material
hurt	juice	lift	matter
husband	jump	light	meadow
	justice	lightning	meal
ice		like	mean
idea	keep	limit	meaning
imagination	key	line	measure
imagine	kick	linen	meat
importance	kill	lion	medicine
impression	kind	lip	meet
improve	king	liquid	meeting
inch	kiss	liquor	melt
include	kitchen	list	member
increase	knee	listen	memory
indicate	knife	literature	mention
individual	knock	live	merchant
industry	know	load	message
influence	knowledge	loan	metal
information		lock	method
inquire	labor	log	middle
insect	lack	look	midnight

mile	notice	pause	possess
milk	novel	pay	possession
mill	number	peace	possibility
mind	nurse	pen	post
mine	nut	pencil	pot
mineral		penny	potato
minister	obey	people	pour
minute	object	perform	powder
miss	observe	period	power
mistake	occasion	permit	praise
mix	occupation	person	pray
model	occur	personality	prayer
moment	ocean	philosophy	prefer
money	offer	photograph	prepare
month	office	phrase	preparation
moon	oil	piano	present
morning	open	pick	president
mother	opera	picture	press
motion	operate	pie	prevent
motor	operation	piece	price
mountain	opinion	pig	pride
mouth	opportunity	pile	print
movement	order	pillow	prison
movie	organization	pin	prisoner
mud	organize	pipe	privilege
murder	owe	pity	prize
muscle	own	place	problem
music		plain	produce
mystery	pack	plan	product
	package	plane	production
name	page	plant	professor
nation	pain	play	program
nature	paint	please	progress
neck	pair	pleasure	promise
need	pan	plow	protect
needle	paper	pocket	protest
neighbor	pardon	poem	prove
nest	parent	poet	public
net	park	poetry	pull
news	part	point	punish
newspaper	party	poison	pupil
night	pass	pole	purpose
noise	passenger	politics	push
noon	past	pond	put
north	path	pool	puzzle
nose	patient	population	
note	pattern	position	quality

quantity	robe	sell	size
quarter	rock	senator	skill
queen	roll	send	skin
question	roof	sense	skirt
	room	sentence	sky
rabbit	root	separate	sleep
race	rope	servant	slip
radio	rose	serve	smell
railroad	row	service	smile
rain	rub	set	smoke
raise	rubber	settle	snow
reach	rug	sew	soap
read	ruin	sex	society
realize	rule	shadow	soil
reason	run	shake	soldier
receive	rush	shame	son
recognize		shape	song
recommend	saddle	share	sorrow
record	safety	sheep	sort
recover	sail	sheet	soul
relation	saint	shell	sound
relief	sake	shine	soup
religion	salary	ship	south
remain	sale	shirt	space
remember	salt	shock	spare
remind	sand	shoe	speak
remove	satisfy	shoot	speech
repair	save	shop	speed
repeat	say	shore	spell
reply	scene	shoulder	spend
report	school	shout	spirit
represent	scream	show	spoil
require	sea	shower	spoon
respect	search	shut	sport
responsibility	season	side	spot
rest	seat	sight	spread
result	second	sign	spring
return	secret	signal	square
reward	secretary	silence	stair
ribbon	section	silk	stamp
rice	see	silver	stand
ride	seed	sin	star
right	seek	sing	stare
ring	seem	sink	start
rise	seize	sister	state
river	select	sit	station
road	self	situation	stay

steal	table	toy	waste
steam	tail	track	watch
steel	take	trade	water
step	talk	train	wave
stick	taste	travel	way
stir	tax	treasure	wear
stocking	tea	treat	weather
stomach	teach	tree	wedding
stone	teacher	trick	week
stop	team	trip	weep
store	tear	trouble	weigh
storm	teeth	trousers	weight
story	telephone	truck	well
stove	television	trunk	west
stranger	tell	trust	wheat
stream	temper	truth	wheel
street	temperature	try	whip
strength	term	turn	whisper
strike	territory	type	whistle
string	test		widow
struggle	thank	uncle	wife
student	theater	understand	will
study	theory	university	win
stuff	thing	urge	wind
style	think	use	window
subject	thought		wine
succeed	thread	vacation	wing
success	threaten	valley	winter
sugar	throat	value	wipe
suggest	throw	variety	wish
suggestion	thunder	vegetable	wolf
suit	ticket	view	woman
sum	tide	village	wonder
summer	tie	visit	wood
sun	time	voice	wool
supper	tin	vote	word
supply	title	voyage	work
support	tobacco		world
suppose	tone	wait	worry
surface	tongue	wake	wound
surprise	tool	walk	wrap
surround	tooth	wall	
sweep	top	wander	yard
swim	total	want	year
swing	touch	war	youth
sympathy	tower	warn	
system	town	wash	

· APPENDIX D ·

QUESTIONS FOR CONVERSATIONS AND CORRESPONDENCE WITH NATIVE SPEAKERS

About School

How far is your school from your home? How do you get there?

Do students in your school wear uniforms? If not, what do you wear?

What subjects do you study in school? How many hours each day?

How long do you spend on homework every day?

What kind of examinations do you have? When? How important are they?

What do you like and dislike about going to school?

Does your school have dances and parties? Clubs? A newspaper?

What do you generally do after school each day?

What are your favorite TV programs? How many hours do you watch TV each week?

About Your Home

Do you live in a house or in an apartment?

What is your building made of?

Is there a wall around your building?

How many rooms are there in your home? What is each room called?

How many people live in your home? Are they all related to you?

Is your home in the city or in the country?

Do you have any pets? If so, what are they, and what do they eat?

In homes where you have visited, do pets usually live inside the house?

Do the teenagers in your family ever disagree with the adults?
What do teenagers and adults argue about?
What happens when young persons disobey their parents?
How were you punished when you were a young child?
Must young people get permission from their parents to marry?
Do friends from different races and religions sometimes come to
   ·your home? Do you visit them?

About Food

How many meals are served each day in your home? What are
   they called?
At what times are the meals eaten?
Who prepares the meals?
Are there meals every day that the whole family eats together?
What table manners do parents want their children to learn?
Is there something that is always said before a meal by one or more
   members of the family?
Is there anything that is usually said during the meal or at the end
   of the meal?
If you need something from another part of the table, how do you
   get it?
Must a child eat everything that is on his plate, even if he does not
   want it?
What kinds of food do you like best? What don't you like?
Which member of the family buys the food? Where?

About Other Topics

Do most of the adults you know own cars? Do any of your teenage
   friends own cars?
Do many people whom you know use public transporation?
   (Buses? Subways?)
How often do you see beggars on the streets of your town?
Have you ever known any farmers?
Have you ever seen animals used for work (pulling wagons, for
   instance)?
In your town, do women sometimes wear clothing that looks like
   men's?

Which occupations have different kinds of clothing?

How many of the people you know work in coal mines or oil
   fields?

How do people learn about health in your town? (In school? From
   radio and TV? From magazines and newspapers?)

How often do you see someone reading a book or a magazine?

How often do *you* read a book or a magazine?

How many movies have you seen this year?

How do you usually spend your vacations and holidays?

·APPENDIX E·

AN INTRODUCTORY CROSSWORD PUZZLE

The words to be used for filling the spaces are listed on page 132. When students have not had experience with crossword puzzles, a simple puzzle like this should be copied on the blackboard, to be used by the teacher and the students, working together, to demonstrate the technique. After that, puzzles may be done by individual students or by small groups.

ACROSS

1. Tuesday is between Monday and ____.
6. I have two ears but only ____ nose.
7. The number after 89 is ____.
9. We hear with each ear, and we see with each ____.
10. This tea is ____ hot to drink.
11. Did she ring that bell? No. He ____ it.

DOWN

1. They were happy when their team ____ the game.
2. What did you eat for ____?
3. You don't like coffee, ____ you?
4. Come back in ____ hour, please.
5. To make green, we mix blue and ____.
8. France is larger ____ England.

ANSWERS:

ACROSS:
1. Wednesday   6. one   7. ninety
9. eye   10. too   11. rang

DOWN:
1. won   2. dinner   3. do
4. an   5. yellow   8. than

SAMPLE QUESTIONS FROM TOEFL
(The Test of English as a Foreign Language)

SECTION 3—READING COMPREHENSION AND VOCABULARY

This section is designed to measure your ability to understand various kinds of reading materials, as well as your ability to understand the meanings and uses of words.

There are two types of questions in this section, with special directions for each type.

Directions: In questions 1-4, each sentence has a word or phrase underlined. Below each sentence are four other words or phrases, marked (A), (B), (C), and (D). You are to choose the <u>one</u> word or phrase that <u>best keeps the meaning</u> of the original sentence if it is substituted for the underlined word or phrase. Then, on your answer sheet, find the number of the question and blacken the space that corresponds to the letter of the answer you have chosen so that the letter inside the oval cannot be seen.

Example   **Sample Answer**

The <u>ordinary</u> land snail moves at the rate of about two inches per   Ⓐ Ⓑ ● Ⓓ
minute.
(A) expert   (B) active   (C) common   (D) colorful

The best answer is (C) because the sentence, "The common land snail moves at the rate of about two inches per minute." is closest in meaning to the original sentence, "The ordinary land snail moves at the rate of about two inches per minute." Therefore, you should mark answer (C).

As soon as you understand the directions, begin work on the questions.

Practice Questions

1. Americans <u>customarily</u> enjoy a large dinner on holidays.
   (A) communally   (B) festively   (C) traditionally   (D) happily

2. The two representatives signed the <u>treaty</u> in front of television cameras.
   (A) letter   (B) order   (C) agreement   (D) petition

3. Because of a recent policy change, all departments are to make <u>cutbacks</u> in spending.
   (A) a redistribution of   (B) increases in
      (C) reductions in   (D) withdrawals of

4. Anthropologists have <u>striven</u> with only some degree of success to make the study of humans an inductive science.
   (A) promised   (B) attempted   (C) expected   (D) pretended

(Reprinted by Permission)

·INDEX·